The Candy Cards

The Shocking Story of Dean Corll

ROBERT BROWN

Copyright © Robert Brown - 2019

All rights reserved.

No part of this publication may be reproduced, stored in a retrieval system, or transmitted, without the prior written permission by the author.

This is based on a true story. No names have been changed, however, some of the dialogue, thoughts and conversations between people have been altered to give the reader a better picture of the events that took place. The views expressed in this book are not those of the author – they represent a dramatization of the shocking Houston Mass Murders in the 1970s.

Disclaimer: The material in this publication has a strong adult theme and is intended for an adult audience.

Reader discretion is advised.

TABLE OF CONTENTS

PART I
THE BEGINNING OF THE END

CHAPTER 1	2
CHAPTER 2	6
CHAPTER 3	10
CHAPTER 4	14
CHAPTER 5	17
CHAPTER 6	23
CHAPTER 7	26

PART II
CANDY MAN

CHAPTER 8	34
CHAPTER 9	38
CHAPTER 10	44
CHAPTER 11	49
CHAPTER 12	55
CHAPTER 13	59
CHAPTER 14	64
CHAPTER 15	67
CHAPTER 16	72
CHAPTER 17	75
CHAPTER 18	80

PART III
THE PIED PIPER

CHAPTER 19	83
CHAPTER 20	88
CHAPTER 21	93

CHAPTER 22 98
CHAPTER 23 103
CHAPTER 24 108
CHAPTER 25 113
CHAPTER 26 118
CHAPTER 27 123
CHAPTER 28 128

PART IV
ENDGAME

CHAPTER 29 133
CHAPTER 230 139
CHAPTER 31 142
CHAPTER 32 148
CHAPTER 33 154
CHAPTER 34 159
CHAPTER 35 165
CHAPTER 36 170
ABOUT THE AUTHOR 175
MORE BOOKS BY ROBERT BROWN 176

PART I
THE BEGINNING OF THE END

CHAPTER 1

AUGUST 1970 – HOUSTON, TEXAS

Dean Corll glared at the youth standing in front of him and shook his head.

"What do you mean you dropped out of school?" he asked loudly.

He was sitting on a sofa in the lounge of his one-bedroomed apartment on Yorktown Street, irritated. The sweltering Houston heat was all-engulfing and streams of perspiration were running down the nape of his neck.

Fifteen-year-old David Brooks took off his glasses and wiped tears from his eyes with his knuckles. "I just sort of dropped out, Dean," he replied in a tender voice. "I cannot cope with Mom and Dad's divorce anymore, you know?"

Dean, dressed only in a pair of shorts and flip-flops, gave a slight nod. "I understand. Come, sit down. Please stop crying." It was a Saturday afternoon and he wasn't working shift today.

Swallowing his tears, young David replaced his glasses and joined the man – who was twice his age, but whom he regarded as his best friend

– on the sofa. He pushed his long blond hair behind his ears and asked, "What is going to become of me?"

"Your parents aren't going to support you if you're not going to school anymore," Dean Corll told him. "Divorced or not. You will have to get a job somewhere, Dave." Staring out the front windows, Dean noticed that the Live Oak trees outside weren't even showing a hint of color-change in their leaves; not yet, anyway. It had been an unusually long summer this year.

"I know," replied David, "but that is going to take a week or two. What do I do in the meantime?" He dropped his head backward onto the sofa's headrest and studied the wooden ceiling fan, where it was pointlessly swirling around hot air, squeaking with each revolution.

"Well," said Dean Corll, "you can stay here for a while... until you find a job, that is."

He felt sorry for the boy.

He had met David Brooks two years earlier, when Brooks was still in sixth grade. Since then, they had become good friends and had often gone to the beach together or spent time at the lake, fishing and making conversation. David had mentioned on many occasions how Dean was the only older man not mocking his appearance, which was petite and somewhat girly.

Dean had become a bit of a father figure to the boy and he knew that young David would do almost anything he said. *Almost*. The one thing he hadn't been able to convince the lad about was to engage in intimate activities with him.

This is my chance, he now thought. *David is vulnerable and in need of cash*.

Being a homosexual man in the early 1970s wasn't easy. Being a homosexual man in *Texas* in the 1970s was near impossible. Too many tough guys who would beat you up for that kind of orientation.

But our relationship is ready for the next level, Dean Corll silently told himself. *No one else needs to know about it. Now that David's parents are finally divorced, they won't give a rat's ass about him anymore. I will have him all to myself and I'll be able to...*

"Thank you, Dean," David murmured, interrupting his thoughts. "Thank you for that. I won't sponge on you, I promise. It's just until I get a job to support myself."

"You're welcome," Dean replied. "There's more than enough space for two people and the fridge is filled with food." He placed an arm around the boy's shoulder. "Aren't you hot in those jeans? It must be close to a hundred-and-five out there."

Through the open kitchen windows, they could hear the cicadas having a field day in the sunbathed backyard.

David pushed Dean's hairy arm away and said, "My legs are fine. It's the shirt and the shoes that are killing me." He removed his sweat-stained khaki t-shirt and kicked off his sneakers.

"Beer?" Dean said, raising an eyebrow. He knew it was illegal to give alcohol to the underaged, but he'd never been the one giving a damn about Texas Law. Besides, he needed a way to relax the teenager for his plan to work.

"Yes, thanks," David answered, smacking his lips.

Thirty seconds later, Dean was back from the small apartment's kitchenette with two ice-cold cans of Budweiser in his hands.

He tossed one to the youngster, opened the other and took a deep swig. Then he sat down again and said, "Listen, Dave, you know that thing we talked about last week?"

"What thing?" replied David, sipping cautiously on the bitter beer.

Dean smiled. "You know... the thing..."

"No, no, no," said David, his eyes growing wide. "We can't do that, Dean. I mean, I like you and everything, but—"

"I'll give you five dollars," Dean blurted out.

A quick sense of shame washed over him. He had made peace with his homosexuality a long time ago, and he had even come to terms with the fact that he had lately been showing signs of paedophilia. *But paying for it?* his subconscious asked. *Don't you think that's taking it a little too far, Dean?* However, all of a sudden, the shame disappeared and he heard himself say, "Think about it, David: five dollars. You need the money and I have the money."

A five-dollar bill was small change to a man like Dean Corll.

Working as an electrician at *Houston Lighting and Power* paid fairly well and he didn't have a lot of monthly expenses. It basically consisted of rent, utility bills, beer, food, gas for his Ford Econoline van, and the occasional piece of clothing.

David sighed, then said, "It's not about the money." Shifting his gaze from the carpet to Dean's face, the corners of the youth's mouth involuntary turned downward.

He really liked his older mentor and friend, but this was a big ask. More because of the fear of failure than anything else. He'd never done anything like this before.

It wasn't as if Dean Corll was repulsive. On the contrary, he was quite attractive. He had prominent facial features with neatly combed black hair and long sideburns (today moist from the unbearable humidity) running all the way down to his earlobes. "A handsome, hardworking and decent young man," was how the people in the neighbourhood mostly described Dean.

David Brooks thought about Dean's proposal for a few minutes and then finally nodded. "All right," he agreed. "But only this once, okay?"

Dean retrieved his wallet from the coffee table, took out a five-dollar bill and placed it on the armrest of the sofa. "Very well, then," he told David, "let's do this."

2
CHAPTER

TWENTY YEARS EARLIER:

AUGUST 1950 – MEMPHIS, TENESSEE

"I'm sorry to inform you about this, Mrs Corll," said the doctor in the pristine white overcoat, "but your son is suffering from a mild heart condition. His blood tests came back this morning and it confirmed what the chest x-ray showed us yesterday."

Mary Corll flinched and clasped her hands over her mouth.

Ten-year-old Dean, seated on a wooden chair beside his mother in the doctor's office, didn't even hear what the man had said. He was studying a life-size mannequin with an open torso – containing interesting removable plastic organs – standing in the corner of the room. The place smelled like chloroform to young Dean; almost like in his school's laboratory. Behind him, Stanley, his younger brother, was sitting on the tiled floor, leafing through a comic book.

When Mary didn't offer a reply, the doctor interlaced his fingers on the desk and said, "It's really not that serious, but we will have to monitor the condition while he is going through adolescence."

Dean's mother finally responded with, "What caused it, Doctor?"

"Well," replied the doctor, opening the patient file, "you will probably remember that Dean suffered from rheumatic fever about three years ago. It is my opinion that this indirectly led to the congenital heart defect we have now detected."

Mary recalled the incident very well. It was in the summer of 1947, a year after she and Dean's father, Arnold Corll, got divorced. She had sold their family home in Fort Wayne and moved to Memphis in order for her two boys to still see their father, who had enlisted in the U.S. Air Force and served at an army base in Tennessee. Dean had originally been diagnosed with scarlet fever but when the doctors hadn't treated the infection properly it developed into rheumatic fever.

"What sort of medication are you going to prescribe?" she now wanted to know.

"That's where the good news comes in," the doctor told her. "We don't have to put Dean on any chronic medicine program for the moment. All I'm asking is for you to make sure he doesn't run around too much and that he stays away from sports and other extreme forms of exercising." He held out a piece of paper to Mary. "Here, I wrote a letter to the school to excuse him from P.E. classes."

This last sentence made young Dean Corll sit upright in his chair like a little squirrel.

No way! he thought to himself. *You cannot take me out of P.E!*

P.E. – or Physical Education – was the only class where the boys and girls at school were separated for one hour a day. Needless to say, this presented a golden opportunity for the boys to gossip about the girls and their mannerisms. Unlike his brother Stanley, Dean was shy and a bit of a loner, and the only time he actually bonded with the other boys in school was during P.E. classes.

His mother gave a sigh of relief. "That is good news, thank you, Doctor. Anything else?"

"I will require you to come in for quarterly check-ups, at least until he is sixteen."

"We can certainly do that, Doctor. We live just up the road," she said and then frowned. "Will the medical insurance cover all these check-ups?"

The doctor consulted the patient file again and nodded his head. "Sure. Unless any of the family members requires additional medical care during the year, there should be more than enough funds available."

After thanking the good doctor for a second time, Mary Corll left the office with her two boys holding her hands, Dean on the right and Stanley on the left.

Once they were outside, Stanley, the extrovert between the brothers, asked: "What's wrong with big Dean, Mama?"

She looked down at her youngest and said, "It's not serious, Stanley. Dean only has a little scratch on his heart." She felt a lump in her throat when she turned to Dean and added, "But he has to be very watchful, otherwise the scratch can turn into a cut and we don't want that now, do we, Dean?"

"No, Mama," Dean replied solemnly. He was still not happy about the letter his mother had folded so carefully and stashed in her fake leather purse earlier – the letter that was going to prevent him from going to P.E. classes.

They walked the eight blocks back to the trailer park where Mary's humble trailer home stood on a set of clay bricks. She was struggling to make ends meet and Arnold's monthly allowance to the boys was only helping a little. She made a promise to herself, there and then, to take on a second job as soon as she could find one.

Back at their trailer, Mary ordered the boys to take a shower and then made herself a strong cup of instant coffee.

Leaning against the door, her mind wandered back to her and Arnold's turbulent marriage.

She still believed that it was ultimately the boys that had driven them apart. Arnold had always been a strict disciplinarian who punished his sons harshly for even the smallest of mistakes. She, on the other hand, was extremely protective of Dean and Stanley. Whenever she had questioned her ex-husband's methods of punishment, it would end up in a bitter fight, leaving the boys crying even harder while listening to their parents screaming and shouting at each other.

Now she was a single mother and life was tough; not only financially but also emotionally. It was quite difficult to raise two boys who were so different in nature. Stanley was outgoing and talkative, a social butterfly, whereas Dean was quiet and withdrawn, preferring to stay inside and listen to the radio instead of playing with other children. And now she had to deal with his newly-diagnosed heart condition on top of everything. She had always regarded her eldest son as a gift – since he was born on Christmas Eve, back in 1939 – but following this afternoon's visit to the doctor, she wasn't so sure about that anymore.

"Mama?" Dean interrupted her thoughts.

Mary looked up and saw his fragile figure, standing there in his too-small superman-motif pyjamas, clutching a postcard and a pencil in his hands.

"Yes, dear?" she replied quietly.

"Can I write to Daddy?" Dean asked, cocking his head to the side.

"Of course you can, my angel. Do you want me to help you?"

Dean shook his head, then sat down at the only table in the trailer home and began to write:

Dear Daddy,
The docter says I have a broken hart.
But you don't have to worrie, because he says it's not serious.
I am not allowed to go to P.E. any more and that is kind of sad. But I will see if there is something else I can do at school instead.
I love you and I cannot wait to see you in 2 weeks.
Greetings,
Your big son,
Dean Corll.

***

CHAPTER 3

SEPTEMBER 1970 – HOUSTON, TEXAS

A month after Dean Corll had his first intimate experience with David, he was driving back from work in his white Ford Econoline van on a mild Friday afternoon, thinking about his young friend.

David Brooks had stayed at Dean's apartment during the first two weeks of September, until he'd found a job at a supermarket and moved back to his mother's house. During those two weeks, Corll and Brooks had been intimate a number of times but, as he was now recalling the encounters, Dean Corll had felt completely unsatisfied.

Last night, however, he had figured out what the problem was. Problems, actually; plural.

There were two major issues. One: he knew David too well – the excitement of their encounters had been diminished somewhat because of their familiarity. Two: Dean wasn't in control of the situation – because he had to pay David money for the interaction, it felt to him as if the youth was in control instead of him.

Driving down South Voss Road in Uptown Houston, with the van's windows rolled down, Dean was now on the lookout for fresh blood. He hadn't heard from David in more than ten days.

When he stopped at the intersection where Westheimer Road crossed South Voss, he couldn't believe his luck. There was a teenage hitchhiker standing on the sidewalk, looking for a ride. He was wearing a black shirt and black jeans with a white baseball cap, and a dirty blue backpack was draped over his narrow shoulders.

"Hey there," Dean greeted through the open window.

The teenager took off his cap and said, "Afternoon, mister. Are you going in the direction of the Braeswood Place district by any chance?" His chestnut hair was short at the back and the sides, with a long fringe obscuring his eyes.

"Hop in," Dean told him, patting the leather seat with his hand, "Braeswood is just a couple of miles from my place."

Getting in on the passenger side of the van, the boy placed his backpack on the seat between them and extended his hand. "I'm Jeffrey. Thanks for the ride."

"Dean Corll, nice to meet you, Jeffrey. Where are you from?"

"I'm originally from here, but I'm actually a freshman at the University of Texas in Austin. I'm in town for the weekend to visit my girlfriend."

Smiling brightly, Dean asked, "Is she living in Braeswood?"

"No, she's up in Dyersdale," replied Jeffrey. "Braeswood is where my parents live. I first have to get cleaned up before I pay her a visit."

"I see," Dean said. He could smell marijuana on the youth's clothing.

They drove in silence for a while, until they reached Yorktown Street. Dean slowed down and spoke in a soft voice: "Listen, Jeffrey, that is my apartment up ahead. We just have to make a quick stop before I take you to your parents' house, okay?"

"No problem," replied Jeffrey, "I'll wait in the van."

Dean turned into the driveway of the apartment blocks at 3300 Yorktown Street and switched off the ignition. "Why don't you come in for a minute?" he suggested. "We could share a joint and I have some beer in the fridge."

Jeffrey seemed hesitant but he climbed out anyway and followed Dean inside, leaving his backpack on the Ford's seat. Glancing at his wristwatch, he noticed that it wasn't even 5 p.m. yet. He only had to meet his girlfriend at eight o'clock that evening – more than enough time for a beer and smoke. Behind him, dusk was approaching and a slight breeze was sweeping orange-brown autumn leaves over the sidewalk and into the quiet street.

***

"Are you hungry?" Dean Corll asked as they walked into the lounge. He stared at the slender boy's frame. Jeffrey appeared to be undernourished but other than that he looked healthy.

"No, thanks," replied Jeffrey, "but I will take you up on that beer offer."

Dean fetched a couple of Budweisers from the refrigerator in the kitchenette, then lit a thin marijuana joint and shared it with his new acquaintance while asking him out about his girlfriend.

Less than fifteen minutes later, he began to make sexual advances toward Jeffrey. When Jeffrey pushed him away, Dean completely lost it. He punched the boy hard in the face and rushed to the television cabinet where he retrieved a length of nylon rope.

Jeffrey was still on the floor, clutching his bleeding nose, when Dean overpowered him and tied his hands together with the rope. He was much stronger than the teenager and it made him feel superior and in control. Jeffrey kept on screaming, "No! Somebody, help! Please!" but Dean grabbed a cloth serviette from the coffee table and shoved it into his mouth to keep him quiet.

He punched Jeffrey a second time, this blow landing on the boy's temple, knocking him out cold.

As Jeffrey's limp body fell to the floor, face down, a rush of adrenalin poured over Dean Corll. He was in charge now, unlike when he'd been with David Brooks.

When he tried to sodomize Jeffrey shortly after the punch, the youngster awoke and made a loud grunting noise before spitting out the cloth gag on the carpet. He started screaming again, striking at his attacker with his legs.

Dean jumped up and dashed back to the TV cabinet to get more rope and a roll of duct tape.

"HELP!" Jeffrey yelled, "SOMEBODY, HELP! HEL–"

Then the cloth serviette was back in his mouth and Dean taped it shut with the duct tape.

Cursing under his breath, he tied his captive's ankles together with the rope.

Unable to control his desire to overpower the youth, Dean wrapped his strong hands around Jeffrey's throat and began to squeeze as hard as he could.

When he finally rose to his feet, he kicked Jeffrey in the ribs. "Wake up," he instructed.

The teenager didn't move.

Dean crouched down and slapped him in the face. "I said, wake up!"

Jeffrey's body remained motionless.

And then Dean Corll realized what had happened, in horror.

He had strangled the boy to death.

He had killed a human being.

CHAPTER 4

TWENTY YEARS EARLIER:

SEPTEMBER 1950 – MEMPHIS, TENESSEE

With his eleventh birthday coming up in three months, Dean was excited for the first time in weeks.

His father had quit the army and moved back in with them. Before this, Dean and Stanley had been left with babysitters on most evenings, while Mary had been looking for a second job.

The trailer home was now getting a little crowded, with four people living there instead of three, but his parents were talking about getting married again and moving to an apartment. For Dean, all of this resembled a silver lining around the cloud of being "banned" from attending P.E. classes. He had become even more of a loner at school, since the other boys now ridiculed him for not being able to take part in physical exercise.

When he and Stanley came home from school one cloudy autumn afternoon, their mother and father sat them down on the patch of lawn outside the trailer and explained the latest plan.

"We're moving to Pasadena, boys," Mary said, showing off her shiny new ring. "Your father and I got remarried this morning and we just found out that one of his old friends offered him a job as an electrician in town."

Dean's eyelids fluttered. "Where is Pasadena, Mama?"

"It's in another state," Mary explained. "A place called Texas. The town is about five hundred miles from here and it's by the sea."

"By the sea?" seven-year-old Stanley exclaimed. He'd never seen the ocean before, not from what he could recall.

"Yes, my son," Arnold said, ruffling the boy's hair. "We will go to the beach on weekends and I'll show the two of you how to build a proper sandcastle."

"Yippee!" the two boys cried in unison, jumping up and down in excitement.

***

A week later, the family had settled in a spacious rental apartment in the city center of Pasadena and the boys were attending a new school.

One morning, Dean was sitting on the steps outside the school's gym, doing homework, when the music teacher walked past.

"You're the new kid, right?" she said, frowning. "Dean Corll?"

Dean stood up and replied, "Yes, ma'am. My brother is Stanley Corll."

"Why aren't you in P.E. class?" she asked.

"I have a ... I have a heart condition, Miss," said Dean. "The doctor told my mama that it is dangerous for me to do physical exercise."

The music teacher made a sad face. "Poor child," she muttered. Then her eyes lit up and she said, "Dean, would you like to learn how to play a musical instrument?"

Thinking about this for a while, he finally nodded. "What instrument, Miss?"

"The trombone," she replied, smiling.

"What is a trombone?" Dean asked.

"It's almost like a trumpet, but with a much richer sound because it has this sliding mechanism." She motioned with her hands to demonstrate the back-and-forth movement.

"Oh yes, I know it!" he said enthusiastically. "It's the one they always use in the marching bands."

The music teacher clutched her hands together. "Exactly, Dean. That's exactly the one. Come, let me show you."

She led him to the music class, feeling pleased. She'd been struggling to find trombone players for months and now she had a boy who seemed eager to learn. Behind her, Dean Corll was babbling along, talking about a marching band he had seen on television once, when President Truman attended a U.S. Navy parade.

A year later, Dean was the school's best trombone player and the brass band he played in went on to win a few competitions across the state of Texas.

CHAPTER 5

Right after he had killed Jeffrey (he still didn't know what the teenager's last name was) Dean Corll got back into his van and drove to the local hardware store where he bought a bag of lime powder and a large roll of transparent plastic sheeting.

Back in his apartment, he removed the youth's long-sleeved shirt by cutting it with a pair of scissors. Jeffrey's body was now completely naked, barring a pair of black socks. His hands and feet were still bound and the cotton gag was still in his mouth, taped shut with the duct tape.

Dean rolled out a four-yard stretch of the plastic sheeting on the carpet and covered it in lime powder. Then he lifted Jeffrey's lifeless body, placed it on the sheet and rolled it up like a pūpae.

What have you done, you stupid imbecile? he thought, staring at the dead teenager in his lounge.

What if someone finds out you murdered this boy?

They will sentence you to death, you know?

However, in the back of his mind, he was somewhat thrilled. The idea of being in control to the extent of taking someone else's life was mindboggling and strangely exhilarating.

He waited until close to midnight before placing the rolled-up body in a sleeping bag and loading it into his van, together with a garden shovel.

Driving to High Island Beach to dump the corpse, Dean's mind was crowded with memories from his childhood. High Island Beach was where his father had taught him and Stanley how to build a sandcastle that could last for three days. It was also the beach where his brass band had won their first state trophy in 1951. He knew the place like the back of his hand.

Upon reaching the stretch of beach sand, he drove alongside it until he reached a large black boulder he had once used as a hiding place when he played hide-and-seek with his brother. Stanley hadn't been able to find him for over twenty minutes on that particular day.

After parking his van on the shoulder of the road, Dean Corll took out the shovel, glanced around to make sure nobody was around, then walked the thirty yards to the spot. The boulder had a bit of an indentation on the side facing away from the ocean and Dean started digging beneath the dent. With a three-quarter moon providing enough illumination in the cloudless night sky, he didn't need the flashlight he had thrown into the Ford's glove compartment earlier.

An hour later – when the hole was about four or five feet deep – he finally returned to his white van to fetch the dead body.

The beach was mostly deserted but he'd had to cease digging on two occasions: once when a young couple had stopped to take pictures of the moon's reflection on the sea, and once when a state trooper drove by slowly in a marked police vehicle, probably on a routine inspection. On neither of the occasions did any of the passers-by see Dean Corll. Whenever he noticed headlights, he lay down flat on his stomach in the shadow of the boulder.

He removed the body from the sleeping bag and hauled it to the boulder as quickly as he could. He was surprized by the tremendous dead weight and he struggled to regain his breath once the corpse was in the hole. Before refilling it with sand, he returned to the van to fetch Jeffrey's blue backpack. After adding the backpack to the body in the hole, he covered it with sand, making sure to compact each one-foot layer with his boots.

By the time he was finished, the tide had turned to low and the North Atlantic Ocean's waves were rumbling in the distance. Even with springtide, the water would never reach the boulder for the next three years.

Dean arrived back at his apartment shortly after two in the morning and slept well into Saturday, which he spent indoors, thinking about his crime. The more he played it over in his head, the more it exhilarated him. He had never felt so powerful in his life.

On Sunday morning, when he drove to the supermarket to buy the morning newspaper, he received a bit of a shock. The entire neighbourhood was covered in missing person notices. They were on trees, lamp posts, buildings and palisades, all reading the same:

MISSING: Jeffrey Konen. Last seen in Uptown Houston. $1000 Reward.

There was a black-and-white headshot photo of Jeffrey, displaying his bright eyes and contagious smile. At first, Dean felt a little remorse but then his cold, analytical mind kicked in and he began to think about the future. *You will have to be more careful next time, Dean Corll*, the voice inside his head told him.

That was when he came up with the "Postcard Plan".

***

On Sunday, December 13th 1970, ten weeks after he had buried the body of Jeffrey Konen under the boulder on High Island Beach, Dean encountered two teenage boys at a religious rally in the Heights, west of downtown Houston. It was a little after 8 p.m. on a cold and misty night.

Jimmy Glass and Danny Yates came out of the church (called the Evangelistic Temple) and noticed Dean's white Ford Econoline van where it was parked in the street. Dean was leaning against the van's bonnet when he said, "Hey, you guys. Care for some free beer?"

The two teenagers approached him and introduced themselves but they were still cautious. "Why would you just give us free beer?" asked Jimmy, who was wearing a brown leather jacket over a paisley shirt, with a leather necklace threaded through plastic beads around his neck.

"Because I'm a nice dude," Dean Corll replied, smiling.

When he noticed how Danny – his dark, curly hair in stark contrast with his white sweater – frowned, Dean added: "And I could use some company. I got fired from my job yesterday."

"Where is the beer?" Jimmy wanted to know.

"Here in the van," Dean replied, patting the Ford's cold metal fender. "And I have more at my apartment, if you'd like to join me. I will drop you off at your respective houses afterwards. Where do you guys live?"

"We're both from Spring Branch," Danny declared, his blue eyes twitching.

Jimmy elbowed his friend in the ribs, but Danny turned to face him and said, "Come on, James. Don't be such a party-pooper. It will be fun! Let's live a little."

After reluctantly agreeing, Jimmy Glass followed Danny Yates into the van and Dean handed them each a can of beer and a business card. "That is where I used to work," he lied. "Write down your home addresses on the back of the cards and I'll show you a secret later on."

Too young, dumb and curious to care, Danny and Jimmy wrote their addresses on the cards as instructed. When Dean stopped in front of his Yorktown Street apartment fifteen minutes later, they had polished two beers each already.

Once they were on the inside, Dean offered them more beer and within an hour the two boys – who weren't used to drinking alcohol – were so drunk that they could barely stand up straight.

Unlike in the case of Jeffrey Konen, Dean was prepared for the assault this time. He had bought four sets of handcuffs at a sex shop in town the previous day, and he'd found a large plywood board in his rental boatshed on Silver Bell Street.

"Let me show you something," he told the two stumbling boys.

Danny and Jimmy were taken into his bedroom where the plywood board was standing against the wall at a seventy-degree angle, almost upright. There were a number of holes in it, from which the handcuffs and several lengths of nylon rope were dangling.

Dean placed his hands on the teenagers' shoulders and said, "This is my procedure board. If you'll allow me to attach you to it, I will show you an impressive trick."

Too inebriated to understand the consequences of their actions, Jimmy and Danny agreed and a few minutes later they were handcuffed and tied to the torture board.

When they realized Dean wasn't in a hurry to let them loose, the boys began to panic.

"What are you doing?" Jimmy slurred, his breath thick with sour beer fumes. "What are you going to do to us?"

"It's just a little game," Dean replied. "Relax and you might enjoy it."

Danny started crying. "No!" he protested, "I want to go home!"

"Shut the fuck up, you sissy," Dean hissed. He retrieved a roll of duct tape from the bedside table and taped both their mouths shut.

While he was doing this, Dean's blood turned cold when a voice from behind said, "What the hell?"

Dean swung around to see that it was David Brooks. He had given David a key when he was still living in the apartment.

"David, what are you doing here?" he exclaimed. "I'm just having a bit of fun, man."

But David wasn't paying attention anymore. He was already bolting out of the room, heading for the front door.

Going after his young friend, Dean only made it to the lounge before realizing it was a futile exercise. He could hear the engine of the teenager's motorcycle roaring away in the street.

After locking the front door, he returned to the bedroom, where he raped and sodomized Jimmy Glass and Danny Yates before strangling them both to death with an electrical cord.

Later that night, he loaded the two bodies into his van and drove to his boat shed storage facility on Silver Bell Street. The shed was basically a steel container-like structure, without a floor.

He dug up the soil and buried the naked bodies beneath the ground, covering them in lime powder. Jimmy and Danny's clothes were stashed in a black refuse bag and left in the locked shed.

Upon returning to his apartment, Dean studied the two business cards where the boys had written their addresses on. Then he wrote a postcard to Jimmy's family, carefully copying the young boy's handwriting:

Dear Mom and Dad,

I have found a nice job in Austin, so I'm dropping out of school.

The job is at a youth hostel, therefor I'm getting free boarding and food, don't worry.

I will visit when I get a chance.

Love,

Jimmy

He did the same for the family of Danny Yates and mailed the postcards the following day, on his way to work.

What Dean Corll didn't know, was that the postcards never reached these families. The mailbox he used on Westheimer Road was no longer in service. Nobody from the post office ever came to collect the mail in there anymore.

This caused Dean to be pretty surprized when he started seeing missing person's posters for Jimmy Glass and Danny Yates later in the week. He decided to let sleeping dogs lie and didn't do anything about it. The one thing he did want to do, however, was to manage David Brooks. So, he contacted him and invited him for dinner that Friday evening.

CHAPTER 6

SEVENTEEN YEARS EARLIER:

DECEMBER 1953 – PASADENA, TEXAS

Less than a year before Dean's fourteenth birthday, his parents got divorced for a second time.

By now he was old enough to understand the process a little better and he questioned his mother about the decision on the day of their departure from Pasadena. It was mighty cold outside, but there was a fire in the kitchen of their rental apartment, where they were busy packing Mary's belongings into cardboard boxes.

"Why did you remarry Dad only to divorce him again after three years, Mama?"

"It's complicated," Mary began. She carefully placed six coffee mugs, wrapped in newspaper, into one of the last boxes. "I guess you can call our relationship 'toxic'. Although we love each other, we cannot seem to agree on certain issues and then our arguments get out of hand."

"But the fights are always about *us*," Dean reasoned, looking at Stanley. "Maybe *we* are the problem."

Mary sealed the box with masking tape and then said, "No, Dean, it's not about the two of you. It is the way in which your father punishes you that I do not agree with, all right?"

Dean understood. He also didn't agree with that. He still recalled how his father had kicked him relentlessly in the beginning of the year because he hadn't washed his hands before sitting down to have dinner. Dean had suffered from three broken ribs and couldn't go to school for a full week.

"Where are we going this time?" Stanley asked in a small voice.

"A town called Vidor," Mary told her youngest. "It's close to Houston and I've met a very nice man there who will take care of us."

"Holy shit, woman!" Arnold called from the living room, where he was listening to the radio. "You've met someone else *already*? Jeez, you sure as hell don't let grass grow under your feet, do you?"

"Be quiet, Arnold!" Mary shouted back. "This is as much your fault as it is mine!"

"Whatever!" came the answer. "Just take your stuff and leave, okay?"

Mary didn't reply. She was tired of arguing with him. This time she wasn't going to make the mistake of trying to reconcile again. It was over between the two of them. She would allow him to see their sons once a month, as per the court's custody order, but that was it.

She was done with Arnold Corll.

***

Later that afternoon, Mary's friend from Vidor picked them up in his powder-blue Cadillac.

"I'm Jake West," he introduced himself to the two boys, outside in the driveway. Arnold didn't even come out to see Mary's new boyfriend.

After telling the friendly man their names, Dean and Stanley helped Jake to pack all the suitcases and boxes into the Cadillac's large trunk.

"Where does he work to have such a nice car?" Dean whispered in his mother's ear on the way to Vidor. He would later recall that the inside of the vehicle had smelled like teak oil and strawberries.

Jake, who had heard the question, smiled and said, "This is my office, son. I work as a travelling clock salesman. I drive all over Texas to sell the most beautiful clocks."

"Where are all the clocks now?" Dean asked.

"At my house," Jake replied. Then he corrected himself by saying, "*Our* house, actually. I've been living alone in that mansion for years, but now that your mother and I plan on getting married, you will all move in with me. You two boys will each get your own room."

Dean first winced (*You're getting married so soon after divorcing Dad*?), then grinned (*I'm getting my own room? Wonderful!*) He had recently started masturbating and it was inconvenient with him sharing a room with Stanley. Now he was going to get some privacy for the first time since he could remember.

***

In January 1954, Dean Corll was enrolled in Vidor High School, where he started dating girls for the first time. Some of the other boys in school were what they called "in love" but Dean could never understand the concept. The only thing he was in love with was his trombone. He only dated the girls for their company; they didn't arouse him at all. Whenever he masturbated, he was thinking about the muscled boys coming out of P.E. class to take a shower in the school's bathroom.

Mary got married to Jake West and a year after that Dean and Stanley's half-sister, Joyce, was born.

During his high school years, Dean was extremely protective of his younger siblings and he helped a great deal in raising Joyce. His quarterly heart-tests were all positive and no further damage to the organ was detected until he turned sixteen.

CHAPTER 7

On the evening of December 18th 1970, Dean met with David Brooks in his apartment on Yorktown Street.

Young David was taken by surprize when he walked in and noticed that almost everything had been packed into boxes.

"Where are you going?" he asked.

"I found a nice place on Mangum Road," Dean told him. "But more about that later; let's eat first. I've made us spaghetti bolognaise with meatballs and tomato relish."

After they had finished the entire pot of spaghetti in the kitchenette, Dean poured them each a Whiskey Sour and then they moved to the lounge.

"Look, Dave," he said when they sat down across from each other, "those boys you saw me with on Sunday night... they were... I was just having a bit of fun with them, you know?"

"Yeah, and now they are both missing. What have you done with them?"

Dean Corll took a sip of his drink and then said, "There's this gay pornography ring running all the way from the east coast to the west. I've been paid a lot of money to send those boys over to California to pose for some nude pictures."

David only sat there, listening. He hadn't even touched his drink, Dean noticed.

"I don't want you to tell anybody about what you have seen," Dean continued. "People might form a misconception of me. There's some money for you in this as well, but you will have to keep quiet about it, okay?"

"The police aren't looking for them anymore," David finally mumbled.

This stunned Dean somewhat. "What did you say? Why not?"

"Jimmy's mom told some of the other kids that the police said that they were runaways. They said that both Jimmy and Danny had been seen at a house where runaways often gathered before hitting the road, hitchhiking and eventually becoming part of hippie movements."

"Well, that's good news then," Dean said, relieved. He rose to his feet while saying, "Come here, I want to show you something."

David Brooks followed him outside, where a second-hand green Chevrolet Corvette was parked in the paved driveway.

"What do you think of this beauty?" Dean asked, raising his chin in the direction of the car.

"Your new wheels?" replied David. "I saw it earlier, but I thought it was someone else's"

"It is," Dean confirmed. He took the Corvette's keys out of his jacket's pocket and gave it to David. "It's yours, Dave."

The teenager's mouth gaped open and then he said, in a trembling voice, "Wow, why? I mean, thank you, but why?" He was staring at the keys in his hand, bewildered.

"For you to keep our little secret about Jimmy and Danny." Dean held out an open palm. "Let's take a ride. There will be a lot of cops on the street on a Friday night and you don't have your license yet. Let me drive for now."

Nodding, David gave the keys back and got into the passenger seat of the sports car.

"This pornographic ring," Dean said once he was behind the steering wheel, "pays incredibly well, Dave. So, if you want to, you can become part of it. You will be rich in no time, I'm telling you."

"What do I have to do?" David Brooks asked, folding his arms across his chest.

Dean reversed the car into the street and then drove around the block while explaining to his young friend how the so-called gay ring operated. It was, of course, all a fabricated lie. He ended his story by saying, "For every boy you can bring to me, I will pay you two hundred dollars." This wasn't a lie. Dean was really willing to cough up the money for more potential victims.

David whistled sharply. Two hundred dollars! That was more than what he made in an entire month at the supermarket where he worked.

There was a minute of silence and then he asked, "Why me?"

"Because I like you, Dave."

"No, I mean not only me, why *anybody*? If you get the boys yourself, you could save two hundred dollars every time, see."

"That is the dilemma, my friend," Dean said, parking the Corvette in the driveway. They were back at his apartment. "The boys are reluctant to join an older man. I was just lucky with Jimmy and Danny. However, if a peer asks a boy of, let's say fifteen, to come with him to a party… Now that's a whole different story." He paused for a moment to let this sink in and then played his trump card. "And if that peer is driving a cool green Chevy Corvette, don't you think the boy would want to get in and go to a party like an adult?"

In the darkness of the driveway, David's bright smile said it all.

***

After carefully planning his tactics, David lured his first two victims to Dean's new rental apartment on Mangum Road six weeks later, on January 30th 1971.

The apartment was across the street from the Mangum Plaza, a new building that hosted a number of shops, restaurants, a nightclub, laundromat, dry cleaners and a hair dresser. Dean was at home on this mild Saturday evening when David walked into his apartment, the two brown-haired boys following him closely.

David, who was already eight beers strong, threw his hands in the air and slurred, "Dean, meet the brothers Waldrop; our very first visitors this year!" He placed his hand on the head of the shortest boy. "This here is Jerry, and over there we have his older brother, Donald." David had picked them up in a bowling alley, not too far from Dean's apartment, shortly after sunset.

"Welcome," Dean told the teenagers. "Make yourselves at home while I put on some music. What do you usually like to listen to?"

Donald Waldrop sank into one of the sofas and said, "The Rolling Stones, I guess."

"And The Beatles," added Jerry. He was wearing a battered chequered shirt with blue jeans, while his older brother was dressed in black tracksuit pants and a maroon jersey.

Dean rummaged through his cassette tape collection and found the album *Let it Be* by The Beatles, which he inserted into his cassette player, on side two. When he pressed play, the song *The Long and Winding Road* started blaring from the speakers.

"I told them we are going to play some adult games," David explained, "and that there will be two hundred dollars in it for each of them."

"There sure will be," Dean confirmed. He fetched his leather wallet from the bedroom and took out four crisp one-hundred dollar bills. Placing them on the coffee table, he looked at the two vulnerable boys and said, while wagging a finger, "But only after the games have been concluded."

"What are the games about?" asked Donald Waldrop, exposing a set of too-large front teeth.

Rubbing his hands together, Dean said, "Let me first ask you this: how old are you?"

"Fifteen," Donald revealed.

Dean shifted his gaze to Jerry. "And you?"

The younger Waldrop brother moved around uncomfortably on the couch. "Thirteen."

"There is no need to be scared, Jerry," Dean told him. "I have a feeling you are going to enjoy the games much more than your brother."

"What do we have to do?" asked Donald, eyeing the four banknotes on the coffee table.

"Come, let me show you," Dean said.

David walked to the kitchen to fetch more beer, while Dean led the teenagers to his bedroom.

Fifteen-year-old Donald Waldrop was handcuffed and tied to the torture board while Dean Corll explained the first "game" to the brothers. "It's a pretend-game where a prisoner is not cooperating and the prison guards needs to punish him. Donald, you are obviously the prisoner. Jerry, you and I are the guards." He walked over to the only wardrobe in the room and retrieved a rubber whip.

Donald's eyes grew wide. "You aren't going to hit me with that thing, are you?"

David came staggering into the bedroom with two cans of beer in his hands. Back in the lounge, George Harrison was now singing *For You Blue*.

Taking one of the beers from David's unsteady hands, Dean pressed the whip into Jerry Waldrop's chest and said, "Now hit your brother."

"No, please," Donald was whimpering.

"I can't do it, sir," Jerry protested.

"Look, boys," Dean said firmly, "this is the game. If you don't want to play it, you will not get the money on the coffee table. Now, hit your brother!" He took a deep swig of his beer.

Jerry made a lame effort with the whip, on his brother's back, and then Dean Corll lost his patience. "For fuck's sake!" he shouted. "What are you? A girl? Hit the damn prisoner. Beat him to death!"

The whip dropped from Jerry's hand and he began to cry uncontrollably. Dean manhandled him onto the plywood board, beside his brother, and cuffed his thin wrists. Then he tied the nylon ropes around the boy's ankles, securing them to the torture board.

While this was going on, David Brooks just stood there, watching. He would later say that it was the alcohol that made him tolerate Dean's violent and sadistic behaviour toward the teenagers.

Dean fetched a hunting knife from his wardrobe and cut the clothes from the two brothers before starting to beat their tender backsides to a pulp. "If you don't want to listen, you will feel!" he shouted after each lashing. Between The Beatles tape in the lounge and the thundering weekend music sounding from the nightclub across the street, the horrific yells coming from the young Waldrop brothers were drowned like words under water.

By the time David Brooks had finished his ninth beer for the night, Jerry and Donald's scrawny backs, buttocks and legs were purple, with blood seeping out in places. The screams had dried up and the boys were now trembling and weeping, weak from the punishment their tender bodies and fragile souls had to endure.

After raping and strangling both boys to death, Dean suddenly realized that he had completely forgotten about asking them to write something down so that he could copy their handwritings for his postcards.

While the lashings had taken up the best part of an hour, the raping and killing of the two unfortunate teenagers lasted less than five minutes.

David was watching this frenzy in a drunken haze.

The next morning, staring at the four new hundred dollar bills in his wallet with bloodshot eyes, he would recall how he had helped Dean Corll to wrap the bodies in plastic sheets, load them into Corll's van and accompany him to Silver Bell Street to bury the victims in the boat shed. He would also recall how Dean had told him that the two other bodies in there (the Waldrop boys were buried on top of the previous corpses) were those of Jimmy Glass and Danny Yates and that there was, in fact, no gay pornographic ring, only the sick and twisted mind of Dean Corll.

PART II
CANDY MAN

CHAPTER 8

JULY 1958 – VIDOR, TEXAS

Dean Corll graduated from Vidor High School in the summer of 1958.

He was getting along fairly well with his stepfather, Jake West, and took a great interest in the vast variety of fancy clocks the man stored in his study, whenever he wasn't on the road. A few weeks before Dean's final day at school, Jake came to him and his mother with a proposition.

"This is a friend of mine from Houston," he said, introducing a stocky man in a brown suit. "He is a travelling salesman like me, but he sells candy instead of clocks."

Mary and Dean introduced themselves, after which Jake made his proposition: "The problem my friend has, is not in the toffee or chocolate department, but in the homemade sweets department. There is a tremendous demand for pecan chewies and he cannot find stock anywhere."

Grinning at the candy salesman, eighteen-year-old Dean said, "That shouldn't be a problem at all, mister. My mother makes the best damn pecan chewies in the whole of Texas." He looked at Mary and placed his hands on his hips as if to punctuate the statement. "Don't you, Ma?"

"You watch that mouth now, young man," Mary said, scowling. Then a twinkle appeared in her eyes. "But you're right, I have sort of perfected the recipe over the years…"

And that was how the Corll's new family business, *The Pecan Prince*, was born.

Mary, Stanley and Dean cleared out the garage of their house ("The Cadillac is never here anyway, with me on the road all the time," Jake had said) and started making pecan chewies by the dozens.

In the beginning, Jake's travelling candy salesman buddy was their only customer, but that soon changed. Residents of the tiny town of Vidor walked past the house, smelling the delicious aroma of the pecan nut treats, and wanted to buy. Within a month of starting up the business, Jake built a small outbuilding beside the garage, where they opened a retail shop.

During the day, Mary ran the factory in the garage while Stanley was at school and Dean operated the shop and took care of deliveries after the shop had closed at 4 p.m. In the evenings, Stanley joined them, to package and label the product for the following day's projected sales.

Little Joyce was only three years old at the time and the three of them made turns to look after her in-between the packing and labelling. In the mornings she attended the *Jolly Jumper* nursery school down the road and in the afternoons she joined Dean in the shop, persuading customers to buy more chewies with her glassy blue eyes and cute toddler smile.

Jake began to take some chewies with him on his sales trips and within three months he was selling much more candy than clocks. Business was good.

Walking into the garage factory one evening, Jake West sat down on a wooden crate in the corner and said, "I have some good news!"

"What is it?" Mary asked, pushing hair from her face where she was standing behind a long stainless steel table filled with boxes and bowls of pecan chewies.

Stanley, who was busy reading his sister a story on a bench behind Mary, stopped and looked at his mother. He picked Joyce up from his lap and put her on the floor to greet her father.

"Daddy! Daddy!" she cried, jumping into Jake's arms.

"Hello, my cupcake," he said, kissing her on the head. "Where is Dean?" he asked his wife.

"Dean!" Mary called. "Jake is back. He's got some news to share."

Dean came in from the side-door, leading to the outbuilding, with a shovel in his hand. He shook dust from his clothes. "What is going on?"

"In a minute," his stepfather said, holding up a finger. "What the hell are you digging for again, son?" By then everybody in the family – even little Joyce – had figured out that Dean Corll simply loved spades and shovels for some or other bizarre reason.

Leaning on the shovel with both hands, Dean replied, "I'm burying spoiled chewies in the back yard, otherwise they will be contaminated by insects." Little did he know at the time that it would be the very same shovel he was leaning on that would become responsible for the burial of his murder victims in 1971 and 1972.

"All right then," Jake said, stroking his daughter's curly hair.

"Come on Jake," Mary said with anticipation in her voice, "the suspense is killing us. What is this big news you have?"

"Well, I've been going over the books and our little family here is doing incredibly well for the first time in three years. I am making more money selling pecan chewies than those stupid clocks, and the retail shop has doubled its profits over the past eight or so weeks. I was thinking we could move to Houston."

"Why Houston?" Dean wanted to know.

"Because that is where I'm selling most of the candy," his stepfather told him. "We could open a new pecan chewies shop over there and we now have enough money to buy a few candy making machines in order to expand our product line to other types of sweets." He paused for a while, then said, "The best part of this is that I will no longer be required to be on the road all the time. If we expand our product line, I can stay with you guys and work on the candy business full time."

"That sounds wonderful!" Mary exclaimed.

The other family members shared her sentiment.

***

Early in 1959, when Dean had just turned nineteen, the Corll family moved to the northern outskirts of Houston, settling in a middle-class neighbourhood called Houston Heights.

There, they opened a new shop – not from the garage this time – and started producing other candy variants such as pralines, peanut butter cups and coconut chewies. Jake also hired two new employees: a woman who helped making candy and a part-time delivery boy.

The shopfront was on a busy street in the Heights, with the factory and a warehouse in the back, and the business flourished almost instantly. As the word about the company spread, they also gained more and more regular customers in the form of travelling salesmen every week.

This was around the same time as "The Day the Music Died", when J.P. Richardson (The Big Bopper), Buddy Holly and Ritchie Valens were tragically killed in a private plane crash, on their way from Iowa to Fargo.

Mary wanted Dean to go to college or university but he told her that he was enjoying working for the family business and that it allowed him to spend time with her and Stanley, and that he could watch Joyce – who was fifteen years younger than him – grow up.

Dean Corll was working hard and enjoying it.

He would soon start to enjoy it a whole lot more…

CHAPTER 9

MARCH 1971 – HOUSTON, TEXAS

As the days grew warmer and flowers began to bloom in NASA's hometown, teenagers who would normally be driven around by their parents in winter started riding their bicycles again.

On March 9th 1971, Dean Corll and David Brooks were driving from T.C. Jester Park to Dean's apartment in his Econoline van when they spotted one of these teens, late in the afternoon. They were busy discussing something that made history later in the decade.

"Wow, what a fight that was," David said, shaking his head.

"You can say that again," Dean agreed.

The topic was the previous evening's boxing match in Madison Square Garden, where Joe Frazier had defeated the legendary Muhammad Ali. Dean and David had watched the event together, on his brand-new Zenith color television, but they didn't know at the time that the occasion would later become known as the "Fight of the Century".

"I never thought it would last fifteen rounds," David remarked. "I mean, when Ali went down in the eleventh, I thought it was–"

"Wait," Dean interrupted, pointing at a boy on his bicycle up ahead. "Don't you know that guy, Dave? I swear I've seen you with him before." The teenager on the bicycle seemed to be in a hurry. His navy blue jacket was flapping around in the early spring breeze as he was pedalling frantically.

Staring through the van's large windshield, David replied, "Yeah, that's Randell Harvey. We used to be in the same class at school. Let's stop and hear what he's up to."

Dean slowed down, passed the fifteen-year-old boy on the bicycle and parked his van on the shoulder of the quiet road, fifty yards further.

David leaned out of the window and shouted, "Hey, Randy, what's up?"

Randell Harvey approached the van and came to a halt next to the passenger door. Staying on the bicycle's seat, he planted his feet on the tarmac and said, "Nothing much, you?"

"We're having a big party tonight," David Brooks told him. "This here is my friend, Dean. He has more beer and weed in his apartment than a police evidence compound will ever have. I shit you not. It's going to be one hell of a get-together; all the cool kids are coming. Do you want to join us?"

"Sorry, I can't," replied Randell, squinting against the setting sun. "I'm working night shift."

"Where do you work?" Dean inquired. He instantly liked the young lad. He had seen him from afar before but now, from up close, he noticed for the first time how good-looking Randell was. Unlike many other teenagers his age, his face was smooth and void of any acne.

"It's a part-time job at the gas station over in Oak Forest," the teenager clarified. "I work as an attendant from six until ten every Tuesday and Thursday night."

Rubbing his hands together, Dean asked, "How much do they pay you?"

"Eight dollars per shift," Randell replied.

"That's two dollars an hour, right?" Dean said.

Randell nodded his head, then looked at his watch. "Listen, thanks for the invitation, but I really have to go now, otherwise I'm going to be late."

"Not so fast," Dean told him. "If you come to my place for the party, I'll give you twenty dollars."

Frowning, Randell asked, "Why would you do that?"

By now, David Brooks was gradually losing his patience. He wanted to earn his two-hundred-dollar finder's fee and Randell was being difficult. "Just take the damn money and join us, dude," he said. "Dean is a total party animal. 'The more the merrier' is his motto. We'll phone the gas station and tell them you have a stomach bug or something like that."

Dean smiled at the young lad. "I'm giving you twenty dollars for two reasons. To make up for make up for your shift money and because I like you and I really want you to come to our party, okay?"

"Okay," Randell finally agreed.

After making sure nobody else was around to witness them, Dean Corll climbed out and opened the van's rear door. Randell loaded his bicycle in the back and then got into the vehicle, where he was rewarded with a can of cold Budweiser.

**

They arrived at the apartment on Mangum Road shortly after six o'clock. Dean had stopped at telephone booth on the way, where Randell Harvey had phoned the gas station to inform the manager he wasn't going to be working that night because he was ill.

"I need to use the toilet," Randell said as they entered the lounge.

Dean Corll indicated a white door, to the right of the kitchen, and replied, "Be my guest. It's right through that door over there."

While Randell was in the bathroom, Corll retrieved his wallet and said to David Brooks, "You're only getting eighty dollars for this one." He took out five twenty-dollar bills, gave four of them to David and placed the remaining banknote on the coffee table. "I did half the work, so I'm taking a hundred and I am subtracting Randy's twenty dollars from your half."

David didn't argue. Any money was good money. He pocketed the eighty dollars and then began to roll joints from Dean's extensive stash of marijuana in the TV cabinet.

"When are the others coming?" Randell asked when he returned to the lounge.

Switching on the television, Dean turned up the volume and replied, "Soon." He fetched a notepad and a pen from a small stationary cupboard next to the TV cabinet and wrote the following on the top line of the first page, underlining it with a steady hand:

MARCH 9: PARTY AT DEAN CORLL's PLACE

He handed the notepad to Randell and said, "You have the honor of penning down the first entry into tonight's guest list. Write your name and a short message."

The youth hunched over the notepad on the coffee table and wrote the following:

Randell Harvey – first one to arrive at the party. Thanks Dean!

Dean gave him the twenty-dollar bill and said, "Now I want to show you a party trick. When the other party-goers arrive, you can play it on them."

After pocketing the twenty-dollar bill and accepting a joint and another beer from David, Randell followed Dean into the bedroom.

"I'm going to handcuff you to this board," Dean explained, "but you don't need to worry, I will uncuff you right away. It's just to demonstrate the trick to you."

Randell Harvey didn't object. He was already feeling lightheaded from inhaling the thick smoke produced by the sweet, crackling marijuana leaves. Dean cuffed his hands and his feet to the board, with his back against the hard surface of the wood, and then stood back. David Brooks was still in the lounge, watching television.

"So, what is the trick?" Randall asked, the joint now dangling from the corner of his mouth.

Dean opened the bedside table's drawer and took out a Polaroid instant camera. The electronics store where he had bought his new Zenith television from, the previous week, had given him the camera as a present.

"The trick is," he said, getting the camera into position, "that you are now a prisoner. I can't remember where I put the keys to the handcuffs."

Making a chuckling sound, Randell replied, "Good one. That will scare the others properly, all right." He winced as the camera's flash blinded him for a second. Then he blinked his eyes and said, "Fine. Now that you have your trophy photo, you can let me loose, Dean."

"You do not understand," Dean Corll said, "I don't have the keys."

"Come on, man. The joke is over." Randell was now anxiously trying to free his wrists and ankles from the grip of the handcuffs. "Stop playing games, Dean. When are the others coming?"

"They're not," Dean replied, shaking the Polaroid picture between two fingers.

"What do you mean?"

Dean dropped the picture and the camera onto the bedside table and approached Randell without speaking.

"No!" Randell Harvey protested. "What the hell are you doing?"

He looked at Dean, who was now undressing, and then shouted, "David! Help!"

In the lounge, he could hear how David Brooks increased the television's volume.

Like the other victims, Randell Harvey was sodomized by Dean Corll but – unlike the others – he was spared a slow death from strangulation.

Upon finishing his sadistic act, Dean gathered his .22-caliber pistol (fitted with an expensive silencer) from his wardrobe and pointed it at the crying teen's head.

"I have no further use for you," Dean said.

Then he pulled the trigger and shot Randell Harvey through his left eye.

He rummaged through the dead teen's pockets to find a plastic orange comb and the twenty dollar bill he had given the boy earlier. Dean returned the bill to his wallet and stashed the comb with the Polaroid picture in the bedside table's drawer.

Four hours later, Randell Harvey's body (together with his bicycle) was in the boat shed with the others, and the postcard to his parents had been written.

Dean Corll had murdered his sixth victim in six months.

CHAPTER 10

NINE YEARS EARLIER:

MARCH 1962

"What do you mean you fired the delivery boy?" Jake West asked his wife, furious. They were standing in the factory warehouse, where Mary had just completed an inventory count. The *Pecan Prince* was doing well and nearly thirty percent of the company's turnover was coming from deliveries. Now Jake had to find a new delivery boy.

"He made false allegations against Dean," Mary replied, shrugging.

"What kind of allegations?"

Mary Corll waved a pencil in the air. "He said Dean touched his… touched his crotch."

"That is ridiculous," Jake said. Then he thought about his statement, while running a hand over his chin. "Although I have to say, Dean has been showing a great interest in younger boys lately. Perhaps he has a bit of a queer side to him."

"What did you say?" Mary asked in disbelief.

"I'll talk to him about it this weekend," Jake replied. He had bought a second property – a holiday log cabin at lake Sam Rayburn, about a hundred miles north of Houston – earlier in the year and he was taking Dean and Stanley on a fishing trip the coming weekend.

"My son is *not* gay, Jake!" Mary shouted. Her cheeks were flushing scarlet red and her nostrils were flaring with rage.

Jake left it at that. He knew his wife's view on homosexuality. She absolutely despised it.

Dean, now twenty-two years of age, was eavesdropping from the corridor separating the candy shop from the warehouse.

Oh shit, he thought, *Jake has a suspicion. I will have to make a plan*.

The truth was that he *had* been fondling the delivery boy, as well as other young boys in Houston Heights, in exchange for free candy.

So much so that he had earned the nickname Candy Man in the neighborhood. Even the parents called him Candy Man; not knowing about his paedophilic sexual innuendos in the alley behind the candy shop, of course. They only knew him as the "pleasant, smiling Candy Man of the Heights" who handed out treats to the neighborhood children.

***

On Saturday morning, March 17th 1962, Dean and Stanley Corll drove to lake Sam Rayburn in Dean's brand new Plymouth GTX. He had bought the car only a month earlier and it was his first trip further than a hundred miles with the vehicle.

Jake West was already at the cabin. He had driven up there on Friday night to get everything ready for the fishing trip.

When the two brothers arrived at the cabin – a solid wooden structure in the woods, with a westerly view of the lake – Jake instructed Stanley to go to the closest town, Huntington, to buy more fishing line and two gallons of milk.

As soon as Stanley had left, Jake sat down in a camping chair on the log cabin's porch and invited Dean to join him. It was a sunny day with the smell of fresh pine needles filling the air. Dean could hear how a flock of double-crested Cormorants were grunting as they took off in the distance

"Listen, Dean," Jake said suddenly, sipping on a mug of coffee, "Your mother and I are a little worried about you. We know that you've always been a loner, but don't you think it is time for you to get a girlfriend?"

Bullshit, Dean thought. *It's not my mother worrying about me, it's you. And it's not about getting a girlfriend, it is about the young boys in the neighborhood, isn't it? You want to keep me away from them, don't you?*

"But I already have a girlfriend," he told his stepfather. This wasn't technically true, but he had done some preparations during the week to make it become a reality.

Jake frowned. "Who? I have never seen you with any girl before."

"Remember when I went to look after Grandma in Indiana?" Dean now said, grinning. "Well, I met a girl there by the name of Betty. I was thinking of driving to Indiana tomorrow and bringing her back to Houston so that you and Ma can finally meet her."

***

Dean had lived with his ageing grandmother for a while in Indiana, when he'd met Betty.

Now, she wasn't his girlfriend anymore, but she did ask Dean to marry her earlier in 1962; a proposal he had rejected because he'd moved back to Houston after his grandmother had passed away. Dean and Betty had never engaged in sexual activities, but they did hug and kiss sometimes and that was enough to call it a boyfriend/girlfriend relationship in Dean's mind. However, that relationship had been dormant for more than two months.

Now it was time to bring it back to life.

After Dean had heard his mother and Jake speak about his sexual orientation in the candy warehouse on Tuesday, he had phoned Betty and asked her if he could try to make their relationship work and if she would be willing to move to Houston and give him a second chance.

He'd told her over the telephone: "You know, Betty, I've been thinking about us a lot lately and I realized I'm not getting any younger. I ought to settle down and get married."

"Is that a counter proposal?" she'd asked, laughing.

"No, no," he'd said. "I can't afford to get married right now. All I'm asking for is a second chance. You could move to Houston and we can try again."

"If you can't afford to get married, I can help, Dean. I can also work, you know?"

"No way," he'd said. "If we got married, you wouldn't work, Betty. Definitely not."

"Oh, Dean. You know, you've always made me feel like I'm somebody special. Let me talk to my parents and I will call you back, okay?"

So, Betty telephoned him later that day and agreed to give him a second chance, but only if he could arrange a job for her at the *Pecan Prince*.

That was something he hadn't discussed with his mother or Jake yet.

***

"Well, that's a surprize," Jake said, interrupting Dean's thoughts.

"Yeah, I've been wanting to tell you guys about her," he said to his stepfather, "but I had to make sure she was the right girl for me before I did."

Jack rose to his feet and patted Dean on the back. "I can't wait to meet her, son. Now, let's go and dust off those old fishing rods, shall we?"

"Jake?" Dean said hesitantly.

"Yes?"

Dean also stood up. "Would you be willing to appoint Betty as a delivery girl? I mean, now that Ma has fired our delivery boy and all that."

"Sure," Jake said in a friendly voice, "if your Betty can do the job, why not? At the moment your mother is doing all the deliveries herself. A helping hand at minimum wage would be welcome."

"Thank you," Dean Corll replied.

His plan was working.

CHAPTER 11

MAY 1971

Candy Man Corll's next two victims were David Hilligiest and Malley Winkle. Ironically, Malley Winkle already had a number of ties to Dean Corll. He was a former employee of the candy factory and his girlfriend was the sister of Dean's previous victim, Randell Harvey.

This time Dean acted alone. David Brooks had recently befriended a girl and he went to the movies with her that afternoon.

It was the last Saturday in May, a particularly hot one (even for a place like Houston), and Dean Corll was driving down T.C. Jester Boulevard at noon when he noticed the two boys strolling along the sidewalk, both of them only wearing swimming trunks.

He stopped the van and said, "Hey there. On your way to the pool?"

Malley instantly recognized Dean. "Hi, Dean," he greeted, then turned to his friend and said, "David, this is the Candy Man I was always telling you about in elementary school."

"Hello," David Hilligiest mumbled.

"Jump in," Dean told them, staring at young David's freckled face. "I'll give you a ride."

The Houston City public pool was about a mile further north and the two boys welcomed the gesture. They got into the van – both of them smelling like coconut oil, Dean observed – and Malley said, "Thanks Dean. How is Mrs Corll doing?"

"I haven't seen my mother in quite some time," he replied in a flat voice.

Two hundred yards before they reached the swimming pool, Dean noticed an abandoned baseball field and veered off the road and into the property.

"There is something wrong with the engine," he said. "I just need to stop quickly to figure out what."

"It's all right, we can walk from here," Malley assured him.

Dean parked the van and pulled a tire iron from underneath the seat. Before the boys were able to come to their senses, he smashed the metal object into the back of Malley Winkle's head, knocking him unconscious. Dean had no need for Malley; his familiarity with the boy made him feel dull inside. It was the younger one he was after – the fresh meat.

David Hilligiest began to scream, but Dean slammed a strong hand over his mouth and manhandled him into the back of the van. Malley Winkle was still on the front seat, his chin resting on his chest, looking as if he'd fallen asleep.

Drawing the van's curtains shut, Dean Corll pressed his knee into his young victim's lower back with tremendous force. Then he began to violate David Hilligiest, while strangling him to death with his bare hands at the same time. He continued until he could feel no more movement coming from the body beneath him.

Afterwards, he pulled Malley Winkle over the seat and into the back of the van to strangle him too. However, the power was drained from his hands, so Dean yanked an old electrical cord around the sixteen-year-old's neck and murdered him.

He drove from the abandoned baseball field to his apartment where he spent the afternoon listening to music, with the two corpses still in the back of his van.

At ten o'clock that evening, he drove the van to his boat storage shed to get rid of the bodies.

**

Ten weeks later, David Brooks was reading the newspaper one evening when his eyes fell upon an article about David Hilligiest:

> *Houston Heights – The parents of David Hilligiest, a thirteen-year-old boy who went missing at the end of May this year, have hired a private investigator to look for their son.*
>
> *According to the boy's mother, they weren't impressed with the way the local police was handling the situation. She was told that her son was a runaway and when she asked the police "How can someone be a runaway with only his bathing suit on and eighty cents in his pocket?" they dismissed her suggestion that it was a kidnapping and told her that a number of teenagers had been running away from their homes during the past six months.*
>
> *Mrs Dorothy Hilligiest hired a private investigator who came up with a lead, suggesting that her son might have been abducted by a sexual offender called Chicken Joe, who apparently provides young male prostitutes to potential clients in and around the Houston Heights area. Mrs Hilligiest and her husband, Fred, have since been spending time outside the Silver Dollar Saloon, a popular gay bar in the Montrose area, hoping to see David being taken in or out.*

The article went on to state that one of David Hilligiest's close friends, Elmer Wayne Henley, was still handing out flyers with a reward for anyone who had any information about the missing boy.

David Brooks knew the name Elmer Wayne Henley. It was one of his old friends from high school. He had been struggling to source new boys for Dean Corll lately, but this name now gave him an idea. Up to now, he had only focussed on strangers. What if he targeted some of his old friends?

It was a Tuesday night and he knew that Wayne Henley always went with one of his other friends, Ruben Haney, to the movies. Tuesday's were half-price nights for school kids at the Houston Heights Bioscope. David Brooks never went since you had to show your school ID and he wasn't in school anymore. ("Because you're a useless dropout," his mother constantly reminded him.)

David fired up his green Corvette and drove to the movie theatre, where he waited in the parking lot for just over an hour. It was a cool evening with a slight sea breeze blowing in from the south-east.

When the film finished at eight o'clock, people came streaming out and David searched for Wayne and Ruben. When he eventually spotted Ruben Haney, dressed in a black tracksuit, he got out of his car and approached his old friend.

"Ruben!" he called, "where is Wayne?"

Ruben, a tall boy with dark brown hair and bewildered eyes, came closer and said, "Hi, Dave. Long time no see. Wayne had to run some errands for his grandfather, so I came on my own tonight."

"Which movie did you watch?" David asked.

"The Omega Man," Ruben said excitedly. "It's about this doctor who thinks he is the only survivor of this biological war, except there are also a couple of hundred nocturnal dudes left and they are all coming for the doctor…"

After listening to the film's summary with patience, David said: "Okay, cool man. Look, we're having a party at the apartment of one of my older friends and it's gonna be wild stuff, I'm telling you, buddy. Why don't you join us?"

"Sure," replied Ruben Haney, "I just have to phone my mom; let her know where I'm at."

There was a payphone booth outside the movie theatre's entrance and David Brooks accompanied Ruben there to call his mother.

"Mom, I'm spending the evening at David's place," he told her, and then, "No, no, the other David. David Brooks. Remember him? We used to go to the quarry together when we were little."

Upon hanging up, he turned to David and said, "It's all cool but listen, will there be a place for me to crash? My mom doesn't like it when I get home and smell like beer and cigarettes."

"Of course, of course," David assured Ruben, placing an arm around his shoulders. "We can all sleep on the sofas in the lounge. Come on, let's go."

When they reached David's Corvette, Ruben's mouth fell open. "Wow, cool wheels, buddy. Where'd you get it?"

"From the same man who is throwing tonight's party," David replied, grinning.

***

Dean Corll had gotten hold of two dozen LSD capsules that afternoon and he wanted to test the effect on someone other than himself. That's why he was extremely delighted when David walked into his apartment with a brand new potential victim.

While David put on some music, Dean opened three beers and covertly slipped two of the capsules into one of the cans – the one he eventually handed to Ruben Haney.

"Thanks," Ruben muttered. "Nice place you've got here." He sat down on a sofa and glanced at the front door. "Tell me something, when are the girls coming?" David Brooks had told him in the car that Dean had hired four prostitutes for the party.

"They should be here any minute now," said Dean. "Let's drink up in the meantime. The first one to finish his beer earns the right to choose a girl first."

Ruben Haney's beer disappeared in seven seconds flat.

Instead of waiting for the LSD to take effect on the teenager, Dean opened more beers and slipped two more capsules into Ruben's can.

Fifteen minutes later, their guest was a goner. No matter what they did, they could not wake up poor Ruben Haney.

"What is wrong with him?" David asked with a worried look on his face. "He cannot be out cold from two beers, man."

Dean stood back and bit his lower lip. "I think I gave him too much acid."

"You gave him acid? Fuck, Dean! What if he's overdosed?" David started pacing around and pushed his hair back over his scalp with two hands. "We need to get him to a doctor, damn it!"

"Nope," Dean replied, "he'll come around. But first I am going to have a little fun with him."

David was too sober to witness another sadistic performance from Dean Corll. "You're on your own," he told his older friend, "I'm out of here."

Dean gave him his two-hundred-dollar finder's fee and he departed shortly after that.

For about two hours Dean was fuming, accusing the unconscious Ruben Haney of not cooperating, whilst drinking beer and brutally hitting Ruben on the buttocks and lower back with a baseball bat. He never checked whether the youth actually still had a pulse.

When he finally got bored, Dean Corll strangled Ruben to death with his hands and then followed his usual routine of taking the corpse to the boat shed to be buried.

CHAPTER 12

EIGHT YEARS EARLIER:

SEPTEMBER 1963

"Things are not working out between me and Jake, boys," Mary told her two sons. "We are going to get a divorce." The three of them – Mary, Stanley and Dean – were sitting in a coffee shop in Houston Heights, late one Friday afternoon. Little Joyce, now eight years old, was out shopping with Dean's "girlfriend", Betty.

"We'll be okay," Stanley said, "but what about Joyce? He is her father, you know?"

What's new? Dean thought. *This is becoming a habit now: marrying and divorcing men left, right and center.*

"No, it's not like that," Mary began, but Dean interjected.

"Not like *what*, Ma?" he said loudly, waving around a half-eaten slice of toast. "Not like you're divorcing yet another husband? Of course it's *like that!*"

Mary sighed. "What I was trying to say, before you so rudely interrupted me, was that we're not moving this time. Jake agreed that I can still use the east wing of the house, while he continues to live in the west wing.

That way Joyce can be under the same roof as her mother and father, although we won't be married anymore."

"Yeah, let me know how that works out for you," Dean sneered. Then something else struck him. "What about the *Pecan Prince*? Where the hell are we going to get money from?"

"Don't worry, son," Mary replied calmly. "I have already discussed everything with Jake. This is not a hostile divorce, we're settling it peacefully. There are more than enough customers for two candy factories in Houston Heights and Jake agreed with my plan to open up my own business. He is going to pay half the profits from the *Pecan Prince* – totalling eight years of income – over to me. That will cover the first twelve months' rent for the property where I'm going to open the new factory, as well as buy all the machines we need for the production and assembly lines." She took a sip of tea and then said, "It's been coming for a while now, I just wanted to get all my ducks in a row before telling the two of you."

This made Dean feel more at ease. One of the strengths he had always admired in his mother was her sound entrepreneurial skills. "What are you going to call the new business?" he asked sheepishly.

Mary's eyes lit up and a smile played across her lips. "As from today, I'm not Mary West anymore. I have changed my name back to Corll." She fumbled in her handbag and produced a folded piece of paper. "Take a look at this, will you?"

As she unfolded the paper on the table and ironed it out with her tiny hands, Dean and Stanley's breaths were taken away.

There was a color illustration of a shopfront with a tall signboard, featuring a number of mouth-watering variants of candy, with the words CORLL CANDY COMPANY printed below it in large gold letters.

"That's beautiful, Ma!" Stanley exclaimed.

Dean leaned over the picture and said, "It's stunning, actually. But... but is that? I know... I know that building!"

Mary sat back in her chair and replied, "Yes, it is, Dean." The building on the picture was a modern two-storey structure not too far from the

Galleria, a 600,000-square-foot indoor luxury shopping mall. Both sons realized that there were would be much more customers there than in the relatively quiet neighborhood where the *Pecan Prince* was located."

"We're gonna put Jake out of business if we operate from there!" Dean now said, his voice trembling with excitement.

"That's a strong possibility," Mary replied quietly.

She pulled another sheet of paper from her handbag and unfolded it on the table. "Here is how this is going to work: Dean, you will become Vice-President and move into the spacious apartment above the factory with Betty. The place you live in now is too small for two people anyway. Stan, you're good with finances so you will become the company's secretary-treasurer. You can now finally move out of the house and into Dean's old apartment."

Both Dean and Stanley were pleased with the arrangement. They both gained a better place to live in and for the first time ever they had been entrusted with official titles.

"It's basically going to be an eight-man-show to begin with," Mary continued. "I am moving Betty from deliveries to running the retail shop. Dean, you will run the assembly line while I take care of production and Stan makes sure that the finances and administration are managed properly. Then we're going to hire four additional employees: one to help me in production, one to help Dean with the assembly line, one delivery boy and one cleaner. As soon as the business is off the ground, we will reassess the situation. We start tomorrow."

And that was it.

The end of the *Pecan Prince* for the three Corll's and the beginning of *Corll Candy Company*.

***

A month later the business opened and they started selling candy.

Dean and Betty were still not having sex, but they were seemingly happy in their apartment above the candy factory. Traveling to and from work only entailed climbing a flight of stairs and they were close to the mall and other amenities like the post office, the library and the hospital.

Within a week, Mary had to appoint a second delivery boy and another cleaner.

Most of the junior staff members were high school dropouts, so they earned minimum wage and the company's expenses were kept low by Stanley. In turn, this presented an opportunity for Dean to surround himself with even more young boys, an affinity he had come to embrace without making too much fuss about in front of other adults.

To everyone in the neighborhood, Dean Corll still appeared to be just another regular member of society. He worked hard, enjoyed his role at the candy factory and kept on entertaining kids with free candy – not to the detriment of the business however.

The treats the Candy Man gave away were all duds; either out of shape or with the incorrect surface texture, but the kids didn't care because it tasted the same.

To them, candy was candy, it didn't matter what it looked like.

CHAPTER 13

SEPTEMBER 1971

Six weeks after he had killed Ruben Haney, Dean moved to a new apartment on Columbia Street, also in the Houston Heights area. He sold his old sofas and furnished the new place with a leather lounge suite, consisting of two couches and two chairs. The Columbia Street apartment had pretty much the same layout as the one in Mangum Road, but it was more spacious; the living room was about twice the size of the lounge in his previous apartment.

On a rainy Sunday morning, late in September, David Brooks brought his friend Wayne Henley to Dean's apartment; a place that was now David's second home.

Wayne was a pimple-faced teenager, a few months younger than David, who'd had a violent and rough childhood. Wayne's father was a drunk who had constantly assaulted his wife and children, before deserting the family in March 1970. Now, Wayne was a school dropout and the breadwinner of the house, financially supporting his mother and his three younger brothers by working two jobs.

Dean was busy smoking a joint and watching television in the living room when David walked in and introduced Wayne Henley to him.

"Have a seat," Dean said, indicating the couch beside the one he was slouched upon.

Henley sat down and looked around while David went into the kitchen to fetch something to drink. The new visitor had curly brown hair and his lean body was dressed in faded blue coveralls – with the logo of a local supermarket on the chest – over a black vest.

"So, what's your story?" Dean Corll asked him.

Taking out a red-and-white soft pack of Marlboros from his pocket, Henley lit a cigarette and then said, "What do you mean my *story*?"

Dean puffed on his joint. "That stuff will kill you, you know?" he warned, pointing at the pack of Marlboros on Wayne Henley's lap. Dean rarely smoked cigarettes, he preferred his weed.

"Says you," the youth replied. "You're smoking much more dangerous stuff right there, man."

"Marijuana is medicinal," Dean said matter-of-factly. He instantly liked Wayne Henley. He liked his cocky attitude and he liked the fact that, emotionally, the teenager seemed much older than fifteen.

David returned from the kitchen and handed them each a bottle of root beer before sitting down on a chair across from them.

Unscrewing the cap, Dean took another look at Wayne and then decided that the lad was not going to become a victim. He suddenly had bigger plans for Wayne. Now that David Brooks had a girlfriend, his involvement had grown sluggish and it was taking him longer and longer to bring in new boys. Dean reckoned it was time to recruit a new accomplice.

"I have a proposition for you," he told Wayne Henley, after taking a sip of root beer.

Henley tipped cigarette ash into the palm of his hand, then replied, "What?" in his arrogant manner.

"How would you like to earn some extra cash?" Dean asked.

Shrugging his shoulders, Wayne dragged on his cigarette. "Depends on how much cash we are talking about."

Dean Corll smiled. "A lot."

Wayne kept quiet, waiting for further information. Outside, they could hear police sirens sounding in the distance; something not that uncommon in Houston Heights.

"There is this homosexual slavery ring," Dean explained, "that operates from Dallas to California. These guys pay very well for teenage boys. For every runaway boy between the age of thirteen and eighteen you bring to my apartment, I will pay you two hundred dollars."

"Fuck me!" Wayne exclaimed.

David Brooks glared at Dean, as if saying: What are you doing, man?

"Ask David," Dean told Wayne. "He's earned his fair share of money already."

"What do they do to the boys?" Wayne wanted to know.

"I'm not exactly sure," Dean lied. "That's not the point, however. The point is that some of the youngsters here in Houston are up to no good. They steal and plunder and blemish walls with graffiti. Don't get me wrong, I'm not saying that selling them to the ring will get rid of the problem, but these boys are no loss to our society. Most of them are a burden to their parents anyway."

Wayne stubbed his cigarette out in a ceramic mug on a glass table beside the couch, contemplating this mysterious crime ring the older man was talking about. After about half a minute, he looked up and said, "Let me think about it."

***

He thought about it for more than four months.

On February 9th 1972, a tired-looking Wayne Henley walked into Dean's apartment with a seventeen-year-old teenager by his side.

"This is Rusty from the Oak Forest district," he said nonchalantly. The boy's name was actually Willard Branch Jr. but he had told Wayne earlier that everybody called him Rusty because of his ginger hair. Neither

Wayne nor Dean knew at the time that Rusty was the son of Willard Branch Sr, a prominent Houston Police officer.

"What made you change your mind?" Dean asked Wayne. He'd been waiting all this time without getting any new boys to entertain him. David Brooks was so busy with his girlfriend that he hadn't brought any teenagers to the apartment since August the previous year.

"Financial trouble," Wayne replied, staring at the floor.

Rusty raised his eyebrows and said, "What's going on, Wayne? You said we were gonna smoke some pot here." He was wearing a brown woollen jersey over a white t-shirt and a purple scarf was wrapped around his neck, contrasting sharply with his pale face.

Wayne placed a hand on the boy's shoulder. "In a moment," he replied patiently. Then he turned to face Dean and said, "My reward?"

"What reward?" Rusty's voice was now filled with anxiety. "What's going on here?"

Dean took a deep breath. "Walk with me," he told Rusty. "There is a reward for you too."

Rusty and Wayne followed him to his dimly lit bedroom, where the torture board was waiting against the wall.

"What's that for?" Rusty began. Before he could utter another word, Dean shoved a formaldehyde-soaked cloth in his face and pushed him up against the plywood board.

Within half a minute, the passed-out ginger was cuffed onto the board.

Turning around, Dean said to Wayne, "It's just to transport him to Dallas in my van."

"You do what you must," Wayne replied. "I only want my reward."

Dean fetched his wallet from the bedside table and took out two hundred dollars. "Thanks, you did well," he said, handing the money to Wayne.

Wayne took the two hundred dollars, looked at Rusty's motionless body against the board and shook his head. "I have a better way to do that,

Dean. I'll show you next time. Right now I have to go, okay? Need to pay some debts and stuff."

Then he disappeared into the lounge and made his way to the front door.

It had been almost half a year since Dean had someone on his procedure board and now the excitement totally overpowered him. He slammed the bedroom door shut and ripped his clothes off in a hurry.

***

Fourteen minutes later, Willard Branch, a.k.a. Rusty, was dead.

After having his way with the youth, Dean Corll had castrated him with a hunting knife and then shot him in the head with his pistol.

This was the day when Dean Corll made peace with the fact that he was a psychopath and a serial killer.

The realization came remarkably easy.

CHAPTER 14

EIGHT YEARS EARLIER:

MARCH 1964

"I've decided to join the army, Ma," Dean said.

He had called a meeting with his mother the previous day and they were now in *Corll Candy Company's* administration office. The aroma of hazelnut and caramel filled the air in the small prefab room between the factory and the shop.

Mary Corll scratched her head. "What? Why on earth would you want to do that?"

"To serve my country," replied Dean.

"What about Betty then?"

Dean knew his mother was going to ask the question, so he was prepared for it. He had discussed the issue with his so-called girlfriend earlier. "She will wait for me, Ma," he now told Mary. "It's only for two years or so." Upon noticing the worried look on his mother's face he added the lie: "We're going to get married when I get back."

The reality was that he couldn't wait to get out of Houston and away from Betty. She was growing more and more impatient with his inability to become involved with her on a sexual level and it was now at a point where she would soon discover what he called his "liberal sexual orientation".

"Who's going to take care of the assembly line while you're away?" Mary asked.

"I have a few guys in mind, Ma," Dean said, folding his arms. "All of them are hard workers and honest men. You can interview them this weekend and decide yourself who will be my replacement. I'm only leaving in July."

He was glad his mother had only asked about Betty and his job and not about his heart condition. Although he hadn't been for doctor check-ups in the past three years and felt physically fine, he thought Mary would have remembered about his condition. But it seemed that she was getting old. Her memory was starting to fail her.

Mary rose to her feet. "Very well then. But in the meantime you still have a job to do, young man. Let's get those pralines packaged and ready for shipment. The mall kiosk is waiting, son."

As soon as she turned to exit the office, Dean punched a fist in the air.

That was easier than I thought it would be, he silently told himself. *Now I'll be able to spend some time with* real *men for a change.*

***

Four months later, he clocked in at the Fort Polk U.S. Army base in Louisiana for basic training.

He had obtained a letter from a medical doctor in Houston, explaining his heart condition, and that exempted him from most of the physical training. When one of the officers asked him what he was doing in the army when he had a heart problem, Dean simply answered, "I want to become a radio repair man." Like his father, Arnold, electronics fascinated Dean Corll immensely.

After cruising through the nine weeks of basics, he was transferred to a training center at Fort Benning in Georgia where he completed a number of courses in electronica and communications before being moved to his permanent assignment at Fort Hood, Portland, where he became exactly what he had asked for: a radio repair man.

During the Christmas holidays of 1964, Dean engaged in sexual intercourse with another male for the first time in his life. He was twenty-five years old.

It was a chilly Thursday afternoon when he finished his shift at the radio repair shop and approached the communal bathrooms to take a shower. Two of his fellow soldiers were already occupying the open-plan showers, soaping their bodies in the hot and steamy ten-by-twelve-feet cubicle. One was also a radio repair man (who was definitely not gay, Dean knew) and the other was one of the chefs (who had displayed homosexual behavior toward Dean before).

Dean watched the young chef's masculine buttocks and thighs with preying eyes while undressing and folding his uniform. By the time he joined the two men, his fellow repair man got out and Dean was left alone with the chef. One thing led to another and before he knew it, Dean Corll was having sex with the guy.

"I didn't even know you were gay," the chef said afterwards.

"I'm not sure I knew it myself," was Dean's reply.

For the first time, he had now established that he wasn't bisexual but full-on homosexual.

Though, he would never tell his mother that.

He knew how she hated gays.

CHAPTER 15

MARCH 1972

Following the murder of Rusty, Dean had moved to yet another rental property; a small townhouse on Schuler Street.

It had been a busy time at work and he'd barely had the time to unpack all his belongings during the month of March. After taking leave in the third week of the month, to complete the move, he was now settled in nicely and he liked the new place. His previous apartment was stuffy and cold while this townhouse was fresh and cozy.

The housewarming party was held on March 24th and the only two guests invited were Wayne Henley and David Brooks.

Wayne had other plans, however. Upon arriving at the house, he borrowed Dean Corll's van, telling him that he was going to pick up another guest. While Dean and David started the party without him, he drove to the parking lot of the *Long John Silver* restaurant on Yale Street, where his friend Frank Aguirre worked part-time as a waiter.

When Frank's shift ended at nine o'clock that evening, Wayne Henley climbed out of the van and greeted his friend under the neon-blue fluorescent lights outside the restaurant entrance. "Your mom picking you up?" he asked.

"Nope, I called a cab," Frank replied. "I'm going to Rhonda's." Still wearing his orange *LJS* apron, he had a tanned skin with full lips and a large nose.

Wayne knew about his girlfriend, Rhonda Williams. She was quite a popular girl in Houston Heights. "Let me save you the cab fare, Frank," he said. "I'll drive you to your girlfriend's house."

Frank agreed and as soon as he got into the van, Wayne handed him a Budweiser. "We're going to a housewarming party first," he told his friend.

"That's cool with me," replied Frank Aguirre, sipping on the can of beer. The majority of teenagers in the Heights regarded him as just about the most laidback guy they had ever seen.

The two of them arrived at Dean's place a few minutes later and joined David and Dean where they were listening to music by the Bee Gees in the lounge, both already in an inebriated state.

"What took you so long?" Dean slurred when Wayne opened the front door. Then he saw the youth behind Wayne and sat upright. "Ah, I see."

Wayne introduced Frank, and Dean gave the newcomer a tour of the townhouse, ending in the small enclosed garden at the rear of the property. David Brooks brought out the cassette player and a cooler box filled with beer, and the three teenagers continued their merry little party with Dean Corll outside, under a star-filled spring evening sky.

After drinking a lot of beer and smoking a couple of marijuana joints, Frank Aguirre eventually decided that it was time to go home.

"Will you drive me to Rhonda's place now?" he asked Wayne.

Wayne started laughing, then said. "Wait, Frank, you haven't played the handcuff game with us yet."

Frank frowned. "The handcuff game?"

"I'll show you," Wayne replied. He stood up and went inside the house.

"It's a good one," David Brooks added, his voice muffled.

A minute later, Wayne Henley was back in the garden, holding two sets of stainless steel handcuffs and a dirty old beige blanket. "Check this out," he said, sitting down on the lawn. He first cuffed his ankles together and then his wrists behind his back. Watching with anticipation, the others saw how he curled up in a fetus position and clumsily pulled the blanket over his body. Seconds later, Wayne Henley jumped up from underneath the blanket, his hands and feet free.

"Holy shit!" Frank said in awe, "You're like Harry Houdini! How the hell did you do that?"

"Slight of the hand beats the eye," Wayne told him. "Come here and I'll let you in on the secret."

Frank Aguirre allowed his friend to cuff him in the same way and then waited for an explanation on how to free himself.

The explanation never came. Instead, Wayne Henley opened another beer and sunk into one of Dean's newly acquired bamboo patio chairs. "I suggest you prepare yourself for a trip to California, buddy," he said and then began to laugh again.

Dean stood up and grabbed Frank by the collar of his shirt. When the youth started shouting for help, he yanked a cloth handkerchief from his pocket and bundled it into his mouth. Then he dragged poor Frank Aguirre into the house.

"How did you do that?" David asked once he and Wayne were alone in the garden.

Wayne lifted his shirt and revealed the two handcuff keys, hanging from his belt buckle. Both of them began to chuckle but suddenly stopped when they heard strange gargling sounds coming from inside the house.

"What is Dean doing to him in there?" Wayne asked.

David's face grew serious. "He is strangling him to death while having his way with him."

"What? Are you serious?"

"There is no sexual slavery ring, Wayne. Dean is using the boys for himself..." David paused to clear his throat. "Then he kills them."

"How do you know that?"

"I've seen it with my own eyes, man."

Jumping up, Wayne rushed into the house and started banging on the locked bedroom door with balled fists. "Dean!" he shouted. "Stop it! I want you to let him go! He is my friend!" David Brooks soon joined him, leaning against the door, also requesting Dean to let go of his victim.

The muffled gargling sounds continued for a number of minutes while Wayne and David kept on pleading at the door. Eventually, the door flew open and Dean, half-dressed, came out with his breath racing. "You two are going to help me get rid of the body," he said, tightening his lips. "Wayne, unlock the cuffs, I'm going to fetch the lime and the sheets."

Wayne Henley peeked into the bedroom and his hand involuntarily went over his gaping mouth. There, on the floor, was the naked corpse of Frank Aguirre. The mouth was still gagged, the bulging eyes were turned upside down in their sockets, and the throat was purple-black with bruises. There was a nylon rope noose around the disfigured neck.

After he had vomited in the toilet, Wayne uncuffed the now lime-covered cadaver and watched as Dean and David rolled it up in transparent plastic sheets.

"Is this what you did to Rusty as well?" he asked, noticing that his hands were trembling.

"I'm afraid so," Dean answered. His voice was as cold as ice.

When the body was completely covered in plastic, Dean ordered David and Wayne to help him load it into a wooden box he had used during the move from Columbia Street to his townhouse. Here in Schuler Street, the driveway wasn't as concealed as at his previous apartment, so he couldn't just carry out a plastic package with the shape of a body to his van unnoticed. The wooden box they were now placing the corpse in was about the size of two standard human coffins.

They loaded the box into the van and Dean's two accomplices drove with him to High Island Beach instead of the boat shed to dispose of the body. With more than half a dozen corpses buried under the boat storage facility, it was getting crowded. Dean realized he had to do some rearranging before he could stow more bodies there.

Frank Aguirre, Dean Corll's eleventh victim, was buried on High Island Beach, not far from his first victim, Jeffrey Konen.

Upon returning to the house, Dean fished through Frank's clothing to find the little notebook he used to take people's orders at the restaurant. He copied the youth's handwriting to pen down a postcard for his girlfriend, Rhonda Williams, offering an explanation for his absence at her house.

Like the others, she never received the postcard.

CHAPTER 16

SEVEN YEARS EARLIER:

JUNE 1965

Dean's time in the army didn't last very long. Although he enjoyed the radio repair work and the sexual encounters with other men, he was missing life in the Heights and his job at the candy factory.

After ten months of service, he applied for a hardship discharge where he stated that he was needed at the family business back in Houston. Since his record at the radio repair shop in Fort Hood was exemplary, his application was approved a few days later and he was given an honorable discharge on June 11th 1965.

The commanding officers never knew that Dean Corll's real reason for leaving was that some of the other troops had begun targeting him because they had found out he was gay – a sexual orientation prohibited by the U.S. Army in those days. These "jocks" would come to his sleeping quarters at night, holding him down and pounding his torso with pillow cases filled with bars of soap, leaving him bruised and battered on many mornings.

That was the reason for the big grin on Dean's face when he packed his bags on the morning of June 11th and said goodbye to his acquaintances at the repair shop. He was now free from the abuse and on his way back home, where it was quiet and peaceful.

Upon returning to Houston Heights, however, Dean found out that he was homeless.

"Where are you moving to?" he asked his mother when he arrived at *Corll Candy Company's* premises, staring at the half-empty retail shop and factory from outside.

"We found a much cheaper place over on West 22nd Street," Mary explained. "It's even bigger than this building and still close enough to the mall." She took his hands in hers. "I'm so glad you're back, Dean. We all missed you so much. It will be great to have you run the new factory."

"Does that imply that I am still Vice-President?"

Mary smiled. "Of course it does. Although, I have to warn you, Jake's business is doing well and the competition is quite strong."

We will just expand our product line, Dean thought.

He had already created a number of new candy varieties in his mind while he had been in the army. Looking up at the window where his apartment used to be, directly above the candy factory, he squinted against the summer sun. "Where am I going to live, Ma?"

"Oh, don't you worry about that," Mary replied. "Betty and I have already rented a very nice little apartment in Yorktown Street. She moved in last week and she took all your belongings with in boxes. Corll Candy Company is taking care of the monthly payments."

Little did Mary Corll know that this apartment would become the place where her oldest son would commit his very first act of sadistic murder, five years later...

***

The new candy factory was a double-storey concrete building with large windows and a garden with a patio at the back. The spacious hall on the top floor became the production and assembly area, while the ground floor hosted the retail shop, administration office and store room.

Dean soon converted the patio behind the store room into his "playground".

He bought a second-hand pool table and a jukebox at a pawnshop, installed them on the patio and told the employees of *Corll Candy Company* – now totalling twelve, most of them school dropouts – that this was the recreational area where they could rest between shifts.

The building was directly across the street from Helms Elementary School, so many of the kids came over to the Candy Man's recreational patio in the afternoons, where they would receive free candy, listen to music and play pool without having to insert coins like at *Peter's Pool Palace* down the road.

Because the people in the neighborhood knew Dean Corll as a well-mannered, pleasant and sincere young man, none of them thought it was abnormal that he was hanging out with these teenaged boys all the time.

Betty, who was still running the shop in the front, questioned him about this on two occasions, but Dean appeased her by saying he was practicing for when they would have their own children once they eventually got married.

Betty found this hard to believe. Ever since Dean's return from his service in the U.S. Army she was convinced he was gay. But she had a place to live, a job, and a boyfriend who was kind to her; nothing to complain about. Her world didn't have to revolve around sex, she decided.

She and the rest of the candy company's employees worked long hours, but they had a lot of fun in between. She wasn't going to change that for the world. Even if she had to live with a homosexual boyfriend and never get married for the rest of her life.

CHAPTER 17

APRIL 1972

Just like David Brooks two years earlier, Wayne Henley started to hang out at Dean's house more and more.

Dean fixed Wayne's mother's car one Saturday and when she met him after that, to thank him, she invited him to Easter dinner. She told him after dinner that she was impressed by the kind way in which he treated Wayne's three younger brothers. Wayne, on the other hand, was trying to keep Dean as far away from his little brothers as possible. He definitely did not want them to end up like his friends, Rusty and Frank.

Two weeks after Easter, on the evening of April 20th, Wayne brought one of his friends, Mark Scott, to Dean's house. This was the same day on which the crew of Apollo 16 (code name *Orion*) was preparing to enter into lunar orbit to become the fifth manned aircraft in history to land on the moon.

Mark was seventeen and his blue eyes, dimpled cheeks and blond hair completely mesmerized Dean Corll when he came home from work to find David, Wayne and the newcomer having a party in his smoke-filled living room. Loud rock music was playing from the cassette player on the stationary cupboard.

"You're such a pretty young man," Dean told Mark after they had been introduced, thinking, *I wish I could have you without having to kill you. You're too beautiful to die*.

"Pretty but tough," Mark Scott replied, swallowing the last sip of his third beer. He stood up from the couch, burped loudly and then crushed the beer can between his hands. "I've been in jail once, you know?"

"What for?" asked David. He lit a joint with a safety match and passed it on to Wayne.

Helping himself to another beer in the cooler box on the carpet, Mark said, "Carrying a prohibited knife in public."

"So, what's *prohibited* about a knife?" Dean muttered, taking off his jacket and draping it over one of the chairs.

"This knife was a hunting knife," Mark explained, putting emphasis on the word "hunting" by deepening his voice, "and I was only fourteen years old at the time."

"Hectic, man," Wayne commented from the corner couch, where he was leafing through a glossy pornographic magazine.

Dean switched off the cassette player and turned on the television. "I want to see if the Apollo craft has landed yet," he told the teenagers.

Young Mark, who had been following the mission in the newspapers since the launch, opened his fourth beer with a crack. "Only tomorrow," he informed Dean. "They're only landing tomorrow."

"Well, aren't you a big brain on a bun, hotshot?" Dean said, irritated. He had formed a submissive picture of the youth in his mind, based on his good looks, and now Mark was throwing his knowledge out there. Switching off the television again, Dean added, "Let's see how good you are with our handcuff game then. Show him, Wayne."

Wayne fetched the handcuffs from the bedroom and performed his trick again. The same as Frank Aguirre, Mark Scott was fascinated to the extent that he allowed Wayne to cuff his ankles and wrists. But, on instruction from Dean, Mark's hands were manacled in front of his body instead of behind his back.

"We will show you how to free yourself," said Dean, "if you write a postcard for us."

"A postcard?" Mark enquired. He was now sitting on the carpet beside the television cabinet with his knees pulled up to his chest.

Dean retrieved a pen and a postcard with a picture of Austin on it from the cupboard and handed it to the teenager. "I'll dictate for you, smartass," he said in an angry tone.

"I'm not writing no damn postcard," Mark Scott replied. "Let me loose or else…"

"Or else what?" Wayne joined in. "You think you're calling the shots here, huh?"

"I refuse," Mark insisted.

Taking a step forward, Dean hunched down and said, trough gritted teeth, "Listen to me you–"

Then everything happened at once.

Mark Scott suddenly shoved his cuffed hands in underneath his windbreaker jacket and pulled out a medium-sized hunting knife. He stabbed at Dean, the blade glistening in the reflection of the living room's tube lights, and sliced through the older man's shirt and into his arm. David made a shrieking sound while Wayne Henley flew up from the couch and grabbed Dean's pistol from a leather holster hanging behind the front door.

When Mark stabbed for a second time, Dean was out of reach but Wayne was now standing there, pointing the gun at the blue-eyed visitor. "If you don't drop that knife right now, I'm going to shoot you in the fucking face!" Wayne thundered.

Looking up and into the barrel of the pistol, Mark first began to shiver and then threw his knife aside. "I'm sorry, Wayne," he whimpered. "Please don't shoot, I will write the postcard. I promise."

Dean inspected the wound on his arm. It was only a scratch but he was furious about the cotton shirt. He had bought it just the previous weekend and it had been expensive. He pushed his anger aside for a moment and sat down on the coffee table. "All right, Mark," he said slowly, "let us begin."

Mark picked up the pen with a trembling hand. "What must I write?"

"Dear Mom and Dad," Dean told him.

Mark wrote this down.

"How are you doing?" Dean continued to dictate. "I'm in Austin for a couple of days." He paused while the boy was writing. "I found a good job." Pause. "I'm making three bucks an hour." Pause. "I'll be home when I have enough money."

He concluded with, "Love, Mark," and then instructed the teenager to write down his address.

After Mark completed this, Dean stooped down to pick up the postcard. "Well done," he said to his next victim. Then he slammed the card down, pulled a nylon cord from beneath the coffee table and began to choke Mark Scott with it.

Mark started kicking with his cuffed feet but Wayne was onto him in a flash, pinning his legs to the floor. Dean suddenly realized that Wayne Henley was getting in on the act. It seemed as if his young accomplice was starting to enjoy causing pain as much as he did. He was becoming an active participant in the murder. David Brooks, however, just sat there, watching passively.

Within a few minutes, Mark Scott was dead.

His body joined Frank Aguirre's on High Island Beach later that night.

**

The following morning, Dean Corll mailed the postcard to Mark's parents. This time he used a different mailbox, on South Voss Road, and the postcard actually reached the Scotts a couple of days later.

Dean watched the news bulletin that evening, where a distraught Mrs Scott told a reporter that she didn't believe Mark would just leave town without saying goodbye. "

"He didn't even take his Honda C70 motorbike with him," she said, sobbing. "That's not normal. It is his favorite possession. We think our Mark was abducted by someone."

CHAPTER 18

FIVE YEARS EARLIER:

APRIL 1967

By the spring of 1967, *Corll Candy Company* was running like a well-oiled machine.

There were now twenty-five employees in total and they were producing seven hundred packets of candy per day.

With Dean not needed full-time in the factory, he started a part time job as an electrician at the *Houston Lighting and Power Company*. He worked there in the mornings and supervised the candy operations in the afternoons. Betty was now out of the picture. She had gone to work for Jake West and found a new boyfriend who was prepared to be intimate with her.

The recreational area with the pool table and the jukebox, behind the candy factory, was still receiving a lot of attention from school children and Dean was still giving away free candy. He would also take school boys on trips to the beaches or to go fishing at Lake Rayburn.

Still, none of the people in the neighborhood saw the warning signs.

On a windy Friday afternoon in April, Dean noticed a new kid of about twelve years old, playing pool with the regular crowd of boys, out on the patio. He was skinny with blond hair, wearing a pair of eyeglasses, and his clothes appeared ragged and dirty.

"I haven't seen you around," Dean Corll said upon approaching the sixth grader. "What is your name?"

"David," replied the boy, looking down at his tattered shoes. "David Brooks."

PART III
THE PIED PIPER

CHAPTER 19

MAY 1972

"Jeez, Dean," said David Brooks, "you're becoming like the Pied Piper, man!"

"The Pied *what*?" Dean Corll replied. They were sitting in his van, outside a barber shop in Houston Heights, studying two teenagers David had identified as possible targets from a distance. Wayne was in the back of the van, cleaning his harmonica.

David smirked. "The Pied Piper of Hamelin. Are you telling me you've never heard of him?"

"Can't say that it rings a bell," Dean said in a sinister tone.

"Well, it goes like this," David began the story. "There's this little town in Germany, called Hamelin. Now, a long time ago there was a rat infestation there and nobody could get rid of the damn rodents. Then, one day, this dude with multi-colored clothes walked into town and pulled out this magic flute, which was incidentally called a pipe back then. When he started playing his pipe, the rats began to follow him, see? Then the mayor promised him a thousand guilders to get rid of the rats. So, he agreed and lured all those hundreds of rats into the river on the edge of town…"

David threw his hands in the air to indicate the problem being solved, then continued: "The only conundrum was that the mayor never paid the guy, see? So the Pied Piper lost his shit and started playing another tune on his flute-pipe. This time, the music caused all the town's children to follow him and he lured them into a cave up on the hill. More than a hundred and thirty kids went missing that day, never to be seen again."

Upon concluding the tale, David looked at Dean and grinned.

Dean scratched the stubble on his chin. "I guess I can see the similarity," he mumbled, "but it's a stupid story. Where did you hear it anyway?"

"I can't remember exactly where I've heard it the first time," David replied, "but I always used to tell it to the other kids while playing pool at your Mama's candy factory." With his girlfriend on an extended vacation, he was now back into recruiting boys for Dean and there was stiff competition between him and Wayne Henley as to who could earn more money for their efforts.

"Hey, Dean, whatever happened to that candy company?" Wayne asked from the back.

"It sort of closed down in 1968, when my mother packed up and moved to Colorado," replied Dean. "She probably got tired of Dave's Pied Piper story, who knows?"

Wayne shrugged and started playing his harmonica in a way that sounded like a flute.

"Cut it out, Wayne!" Dean said angrily.

"Here they come," David told them, pointing at the barber shop where the two teenagers were now emerging from, into the bright sunlight. "The tall one is Johnny and the other one is—"

"Billy Baulch," Dean completed the sentence. "I know, he used to work at Corll Candy Company. He was one of our delivery boys, if I remember correctly."

David leaned out of the passenger window and called, "Johnny! Billy!"

The two youths approached the van, then sixteen-year-old Johnny Delome straightened his denim jacket and said, "What's up, Dave?"

"Hey, Dave, hey, Dean," Billy Baulch greeted. He was a year older than Johnny and he had a thick bush of hair (even after the recent haircut) and a lively smile.

Dean raised a hand and waved in response.

"Hello there!" Wayne hollered from the back. His face was hidden in the darkness, therefor the two boys on the outside couldn't see him.

"Listen," David said, "we're going back to Dean's house to smoke some weed and watch The Carol Burnett Show. Want to come with?"

Neither of the two teenagers were able to say no to free marijuana, so they climbed into the van and went to the townhouse in Schuler Street with the trio.

***

After Dean had raped and tortured Johnny Delome and Billy Baulch for nearly two hours, Wayne knocked on the bedroom door and said, "Dean! Let me in, man! I want to see what you are doing."

David Brooks was drinking beer and watching television in the lounge, but Wayne couldn't stand a minute more of the *Carol Burnett Show*. He classified it as "infantile comedy".

Ever since he had participated in the murder of Mark Scott, Wayne Henley's demeanour was becoming increasingly sadistic. He was curious and wanted to partake in the killings. He did not want Dean to have the boys all to himself anymore. David Brooks didn't care – he just wanted the money. He had earned four hundred dollars for finding Billy and Johnny.

When the bedroom door was eased open a few seconds later, Wayne walked in to find Dean smoking a joint in an armchair in the corner of the room. The two teenagers were tied to the king-size bed with nylon rope and their mouths were gagged with underwear, held in place by duct tape. All three occupants of the spacious bedroom were stark naked.

"Are you going to kill them too?" Wayne asked, folding his arms.

Dean blew out smoke through his nose. "Unless *you* want to do it," he said in a voice barely above a whisper.

"I'll rather watch you do it," Wayne muttered back. Johnny Delome made a grunting noise and started wriggling around on the bed. Billy was bawling his eyes out, but it sounded more like a stifled hum to Wayne.

"You know, Wayne," Dean said, "you are already an accomplice to murder. If someone finds out what happened to Mark Scott, you're going to jail with me, my friend. So, why don't you just do these two and get it over with?" Standing up, he retrieved his pistol from the bedside table. "Or are you too scared?"

"I'm not scared," Wayne sneered. "Give me the gun."

Dean handed him the shiny .22 caliber pistol and Wayne pointed it at Billy's torso. After about half a minute, he lowered the weapon slowly and said, "I'll rather strangle him. Like you did when you killed Mark the other night."

"Good," Dean concurred, nodding.

"Do you have more rope?" Wayne asked.

"Just use your hands," Dean told him. "Knock the wind out of him first, then it's much easier."

Wayne tucked the pistol into his waistband and straddled Billy Baulch, who was pinned down on his back. He punched him in the gut as hard as he could, leaving him gasping behind the gag. Tightening his hands around the teenager's neck, Wayne Henley then began to squeeze.

Dean was watching proceedings with thrilled satisfaction.

When Wayne realized that his grip was too loose around the youth's thin neck, he removed his right hand and pressed down on the fragile throat with his left, throwing behind it his full body weight.

While Billy was suffocating to death from the choke, Wayne pulled the pistol from his waistband with his right hand, aimed it at Johnny Delome's face and said, "Hey, Johnny!" Then he pulled the trigger and shot the boy in his nose.

The bullet ripped through Johnny's brain, exited through his left ear and splattered the bed's rosewood headboard in dark red blood. The smell of cordite and iron instantly filled the bedroom.

"Fucking hell!" Dean exclaimed. "You just killed two guys at the same time, Wayne!"

David helped them clean up the mess and – as he picked up one of the bodies to load it into the wooden box in the kitchen – he noticed a sheet of paper with Billy's name and an address written on it, lying on the carpet. "Dean," he said, "don't forget about the postcard."

***

Three days later, Mr Baulch received a postcard from Madisonville, Texas, seventy miles outside of Houston, in his son's handwriting. Dean had mailed it from there on his way back from a training course he'd attended in Dallas the day after the double murder.

> Dear Dad,
>
> I am sorry to do this, but Johnny and I found a better job working for a trucker loading and unloading from Houston to Washington and we'll be back in three to four weeks.
>
> After a week I will send money to help you and Mom out.
>
> Love,
>
> Billy.

CHAPTER 20

JULY 1972

Having moved once again, Dean was now living in an apartment at Westcott Towers, southwest of Houston Heights.

On July 18th, he stayed up all night, rearranging the decomposing corpses in his rental boat shed. After they had buried the bodies of Billy and Johnny at High Island Beach, he'd decided that the location was too risky and too public. They had nearly been caught by a patrolling state trooper while hauling the body out of the van. He now had to make more space underneath his storage facility, since Wayne Henley had promised to deliver a new boy the following night.

By the time he had deepened the graves and reorganized the bodies, the sun was peeking over the horizon and it was nearly six o'clock in the morning. Dean called in sick at work and spent the rest of the day sleeping, getting up three times to vomit in the en-suite bathroom toilet of the new apartment. The sight and smell of the decaying cadavers in his boat shed were haunting him.

That evening, he got out of bed and made himself a cup of tea and buttered toast; it was all his stomach could stand at the time. He watched television and listened to music while waiting for Wayne.

Wayne and David arrived late at night and introduced him to a teenager named Steven Kent Sickman. Steven had large ears and wore his dark brown hair in a brush cut. There was an acoustic guitar hanging from a leather strap around his neck and he was dressed in flip-flops, black shorts and a dirty white vest.

Sitting down cross-legged on the carpet, Steven said in a deep voice, "I don't like couches. My sister and I always park on the floor while we watch television."

Dean was watching Stanley Kubrick's *A Clockwork Orange*, a futuristic film about an antisocial delinquent gang leader narrating his sadistic crimes.

"This guy is one sick fuck," Wayne commented when the main character started raping someone's wife while chanting Gene Kelly's song, *Singing in the Rain*.

"Not as sick as some other people I know," David said, glaring at Dean.

"Shut up, the both of you!" Dean instructed. "I'm trying to watch the movie, all right?"

It was another sweltering hot summer night in Texas and Steven Sickman took off his vest. "It's like a sauna in here," he moaned. "Don't you have air conditioning, Dean?" All of the apartment's windows were open but there wasn't even a hint of a breeze in the air.

Had he not taken off his sleeveless shirt, Sickman just might still have been alive the next morning. Dean was really into the two-hour movie and tired enough to go to bed afterward. However, when he noticed the youth's bare chest, he lost interest in the television and said, "Steven, come with me, will you? I want to show you something interesting."

Steven left his guitar in the TV room and followed the older man into the only bedroom in the apartment. When Dean began to make sexual advances, moments later, Steven Sickman punched him forcefully in the face.

Dean Corll, now livid, managed to wangle the teenager into a wrestling grip and eventually handcuffed him to the plywood torture board. Then he pulled a baseball bat from a bamboo basket beside the bed and repeatedly smashed it into Steven's torso, fracturing six of his ribs as well as his hip bone in the process.

Screaming in agony, Steven begged Dean to stop but his voice was drowned by the equally grotesque yells coming from the television.

After strangling his victim to death with a nylon cord, Dean tied the body up in plastic sheeting, loaded it into his van and then drove to Silver Bell Street where he disposed of the corpse in his boat shed "burial ground".

***

Four and a half weeks after that, Roy Bunton was murdered.

Roy – who had finished his final year in school eight months earlier – was walking to the shoe store at the mall, where he worked as a junior salesman, when Wayne Henley offered him a ride in Dean's van. With his nineteenth birthday coming up, Roy was a tall teenager with blond hair and a vibrant personality. He always trusted everybody he came in contact with and his parents regarded him as someone who was going to get far in life.

He was abducted and kept alive on the torture board for four days before Dean shot him twice in the head on August 21st 1972.

That evening, around midnight, Wayne went to the boat shed with Dean to get rid of the body.

They drove into the marina, past a rusty signboard reading SOUTHWEST BOAT STORAGE, and stopped in front of stall number eleven. Dean got out with a penlight clenched between his teeth and unlocked the corrugated iron structure's two large doors. Switching on the single lightbulb inside the storage shed, he called in a loud whisper: "Wayne, bring in the package."

Wayne removed the plastic-covered body from the wooden box in the van and carried it inside.

On the right-hand side of the shed stood a half-stripped car, two bicycles with flat tyres, and a bag of lime. On the left were two faded blue carpets – littered with empty cans – covering the earthen floor. Beyond that were a number of black garbage bags, boxes, coils of electrical cable and two shovels. Behind one of the doors, Wayne could see a plywood board – similar to the "procedure board" in Dean's house – and a roll of plastic sheeting. There were no windows and the stench of death was partly disguised by the sharp smell of motor oil in the humid air.

"Grab a shovel," Dean commanded. "Let's get to work." He closed the doors and began to roll up one of the carpets.

After dropping the corpse to the ground, Wayne picked up one of the shovels and asked, "Where should I start digging?"

Dean rubbed the back of his neck, deep in thought, then said, "Right here," marking a spot on the ground with the tip of his shoe.

Wayne started spading into the soft soil, but he didn't get far before striking a solid object. Upon investigating, he noticed it was another body, also covered in transparent plastic sheeting.

Trying not to act surprized, Wayne stepped two yards toward the doors and started digging in another location, where he found yet another corpse. "Holy crap!" he cried out, jumping back. He quickly lit a cigarette to calm his nerves and then said, "Dean, let me ask you a question: How long have you been doing this shit?"

"That has nothing to do with you," Dean replied. He picked up the other shovel to cover the two exposed bodies with soil. Then he moved three yards to the left, almost right next to the wall and began to dig. "Come, help me, you son of a bitch," he hissed.

Joining the older man, Wayne also started digging in this third spot and they miraculously created a six feet trench without coming across another body. The trench was three feet deep and just about wide enough for Roy Bunton's dead corpse.

After burying the body, Dean opened a can of motor oil he'd retrieved from the backseat of the half-stripped car and poured the contents over the shallow grave. "For the smell," he told Wayne.

A gust of wind suddenly blew one of the doors open. Thunder and lightning were threatening from the east, they noticed.

"We have to hurry up," Wayne said, "the rain is coming soon."

"We're done here," Dean replied. Then he stuck a finger under Wayne's nose and warned him: "Listen to me, Elmer Wayne Henley. If you ever tell anyone about this place, you are dead meat, do you understand me?"

Wayne nodded in comprehension, dragging deeply on the fourth cigarette he'd lit since entering Dean Corll's boat shed of death and decay.

CHAPTER 21

OCTOBER 1972

Wally Jay Simoneaux was a busy fourteen-year-old boy. Whenever he wasn't attending school, he would ride around on his bicycle, visiting friends, going to the beach for a swim, or pedalling to the Galleria mall to do some window shopping. He simply could not sit still; his grandmother always told him he had "ants in his bicycle pants."

On October 2nd his bicycle was in the garage, however, and he was walking back home from the late afternoon movie show alongside his best friend, Richie Hembree.

They were in good spirits and couldn't stop talking about the film, *Joe Kidd*, featuring a bounty hunter played by Clint Eastwood, their favorite actor.

As they turned into Yale Street, a brilliant green Corvette was parked up ahead. The two teenagers walked closer to inspect the sports car when a guy about three years older than them leaned out of the window and said, "Hey, dudes, my name is Dave Brooks. Where are you off to?"

Wally and Richie introduced themselves and told the stranger they were on their way to Durham Drive where they both lived, three houses from each other.

"Jump in," said David, "I'll give you a ride."

Getting into the Corvette's backseat, the two boys started telling David Brooks about the action-packed movie they had just watched. Outside, the twilight was rapidly being swallowed by the dark Texas night sky.

"Sounds great," David remarked. After a minute of silence, he looked in the rear view mirror and spoke in a soothing voice: "Listen, guys, we just have to stop by my friend's house quickly. I need to pick up some paint for tonight's party."

"What do you need paint for?" Wally asked. "At a party?"

David frowned. "You've never sniffed paint before? It's great, let me tell you. Even better than beer or weed. You should try it. My friend works for the power company, so he has access to all kinds of paint and thinners. You can have some when we get to his place."

Richie all of a sudden began to babble about how he had sniffed paint the previous year, explaining to Wally that it was true: the stuff really put you on a high.

As David turned into Logan Lane, the two boys marvelled at the tall Westcott Towers building with its lush gardens, illuminated by hundreds of lights indicating the walkways and communal areas.

Parking the Corvette in a designated area for visitors, David climbed out and told Richie and Wally to follow him up the stairs to the second storey of the brownstone building.

"New delivery," he called when he knocked on the front door of Dean Corll's apartment. The two teens didn't even flinch. They were too busy looking forward to the "paint party" to realize what David had just said.

Dean opened the door and David introduced him to the visitors.

When he invited them in, Dean was impressed with the new delivery. Most of his previous victims had been a little older than what he actually preferred. Wally and Richie were exactly the type of boys that aroused him. Wally was skinny with shiny black hair and a lovely face, while Richie was bulkier with deep hazelnut eyes and a sharp nose. Both of them stood at just over five feet tall.

"Please sit down," Dean requested. "Make yourselves comfortable. Beer?"

"Yeah," replied Richie, "and paint." He took off his cable-knit cardigan and hung it over a chair before sitting down on one of the leather couches. Wally joined him without speaking.

"Where is Wayne?" David asked Dean.

"He's on his way back from Dallas," Dean answered, while fetching a six-pack Budweisers from the bar fridge in the kitchen. "He should probably be back here at ten or eleven."

David followed him and then Wally spotted a beige telephone on a table beside the television cabinet. He rose to his feet, picked up the handset and dialled his home number.

"Hello, this is Mrs Simoneaux speaking," his mother said upon answering the call.

"Mama!" Wally replied...

Then the line went dead.

"What the hell do you think you're doing?" David shouted. He had returned from the kitchen, yanked the telephone cord out of its socket, and was now standing with the yellowing cord in his hands.

"I'm sorry," Wally whimpered. "I'm sorry, Dave."

"What is going on here?" Dean suddenly asked.

David Brooks balled his fists. "This little shit just phoned his mother!"

"Did he tell her he's here at Westcott?" Dean asked, raising his brow.

"No, I stopped him in time," David replied.

"Well, then there's no harm, is there?" Dean said, smiling at the two boys. "Now remember, guys," he added, "this is a secret party right here.

No telling, okay? What happens in the Westcott Towers, stays in the Westcott Towers."

Richie gave a nervous laugh. Wally's eyes grew wide.

After handing out beers to everyone, Dean went to his bedroom to fetch a can of white acrylic paint and a bottle of lacquer thinners. While he and David smoked marijuana, Wally and Richie sniffed on the paint and thinners. They also drank three beers each.

Within two hours, both boys were passed out on the couch.

Dean carried them into the bedroom where he tied them to the torture rack, gagged their mouths, and molested them for an hour and a half, until Wayne Henley arrived at 10:25 p.m.

Wayne, David and Dean left the boys tied up, locked in the bedroom, and went out to a local nightclub where they partied until after three o'clock in the morning. Upon returning to the apartment, they drank whiskey nightcaps and fell asleep on the couches in front of the television.

The following day, Wayne was the first one up and he went to check on the boys with Dean's pistol dangling from his right hand. When he unlocked and opened the bedroom door, he noticed that Richie had managed to free his feet from the nylon ropes. Wayne lifted the gun on instinct and then it accidentally went off, sending a bullet through the side of Richie's mouth.

Dean came storming into the blood-spattered room a few seconds later. Despite the pistol's silencer, the gunshot had awoken him from his drunken sleep. "What have you done, Wayne?" he shouted. "He's not dead, asshole!"

He grabbed a length of nylon rope from the bedside table and strangled the bloodied Richie Hembree to death in under four minutes. Then he moved on to Wally Simoneaux, taking his precious life in the same manner.

When he was done, Dean threw the rope aside and glared at Wayne. "You're such an unprofessional, you know?" he said, shaking his head from side to side.

Later that night, the dead bodies of the once energetic boys joined the other victims in the boat shed.

***

Six weeks later, on November 15th, Dean secretly murdered another young man: nineteen-year old Richard Kepner. He was last seen on his way to a phone booth in the Heights to phone his fiancée. Neither David nor Wayne knew about this incident. They were both out of town, attending a youth camp for troubled teenagers near San Antonio and Dean never mentioned anything about the crime to either of them afterward. In the end, Richard Kepner's remains would only be identified eleven years later, in 1983.

That evening, after he had buried Kepner's body, Dean returned to his apartment to find a television news channel airing a speech by Pope Paul VI, entitled *Liberaci dal male* (Deliver us from evil). The speech was in Italian but the subtitles were in English and, over the following weeks, it would provoke a massive debate within the Roman Catholic Church about whether Satan was a real being or not.

One of the statements the Pope made was the following: "The evil which exists in the world is the result and an effect of the attack upon us and our society by a dark and hostile agent, the devil. Evil is not only a privation, but a living, spiritual, corrupt and corrupting being."

Dean convinced himself that everything that he had done to date – the rape, the torture, the sodomy and the killings – did not come from his inner self but from this corrupt being, the devil.

"You're going to be okay, Dean Corll," he told himself as he climbed into bed that night. "You don't have a dark soul, Satan has one. It's not you, it's the fucking devil making you do all these evil things. Let him burn in hell, the bastard!"

CHAPTER 22

FEBRUARY 1973

Dean moved to yet another rental residence in the beginning of 1973.

This time it was a derelict ground floor apartment at an address on Wirt Road, in the Spring Branch district of Houston.

On the first day of February – one filled with the promise of spring in the air – Dean was cleaning the tiny garden behind the apartment when the doorbell rang. He was instantly annoyed. *Who could it be*? he thought. David and Wayne both had keys, they wouldn't ring the bell. He hoped it wasn't someone from work; he had specifically taken the day off to spring-clean his new rental place.

Walking into the apartment, he removed the yellow rubber gloves he was wearing and dropped them into a ceramic bowl on the coffee table before answering the door.

A familiar looking teenager greeted him with a shy "Hi there, Mr Corll."

Dean thought for a moment and then said, "Joseph, right?" He had met the boy when he'd visited David's mother's house on Antoine Drive once.

"Joseph, yes," the youth answered, running a hand through his bob hair. "Joseph Lyles." He glanced past Dean head, into the apartment and then rubbed his prominent nose. "Where's Dave?" he asked. "His mom said he's with you. She gave me the address."

"His girlfriend is back from vacation," Dean answered. "He took her to a picnic in Memorial Park, but he should be back here at around two o'clock."

"Oh," Joseph replied, visibly disappointed. "All right. I'll be going then."

As he turned to leave, Dean grabbed his sleeve and said, "Wait. Why don't you come in for a beer?" He consulted his wristwatch. "It's almost quarter to one. David will be back in just over an hour."

Joseph Lyles considered this for a few seconds, then replied, "What the heck. I have nothing else to do anyway. The skating rink at the mall is under construction."

Dean allowed him to enter and then locked the door behind them. "Sorry about the mess," he said, kicking empty cardboard boxes on the tiled floor out of the way. "I only moved in last week and I'm still unpacking."

"No worries," said Joseph. "My room looks a lot worse than this."

After fetching two beers from the kitchen, Dean escorted the youngster out into the backyard and invited him to sit down on a new wooden bench he had bought for the garden. Joseph opened the can of beer and took a big gulp, before Dean took a seat next to him and said, "Listen, Joseph, have you ever tried it with another man?"

"Tried what?" Joseph replied.

"You know…" Dean put his beer down between his feet and pinched the teenager's cheek with his left thumb and index finger.

Joseph suddenly snapped his head to the right, opened his mouth and sank his teeth into Dean's hand.

"OUCH!" Dean shouted. Then he drew back his right hand in a tight fist and punched Joseph as hard as he could on the cheekbone. He heard a sharp crackle as it broke under his knuckles.

Joseph's head reeled sideways and he screamed in agony. Before he could recover, Dean hit him again, this time on the soft area between his temple and eardrum. The force of the second blow made his head connect a tree behind him with such force that his skull split open.

Dean watched as Joseph's eyes rolled back in their sockets, before the lids involuntarily closed over them. His chin fell to his chest and then the can of beer dropped from Joseph's hands, as his arms went limp in his lap.

***

While this was going on at Wirt Road, David Brooks wasn't having a picnic at all. He was, in fact, nowhere near Memorial Park (or his girlfriend for that matter). He was sitting in a Jack in the Box fast food restaurant in the Galleria mall, explaining his dilemma to Wayne Henley.

"What do you mean she is pregnant?" Wayne asked.

David shrugged. "She's my girlfriend, Wayne. We have sex every now and again, you know?"

"Yeah, I understand that, but don't you use condoms?"

"It's not the same, you know it."

A plump waitress in a red apron momentarily interrupted them to take their orders.

After studying the laminated menu on the table briefly, Wayne said, "I'll have a cheeseburger with fries and a strawberry milkshake, thanks."

"Same for me," David told the waitress.

When she was out of sight again, Wayne said, "So, what are you going to do now, buddy?"

David produced a tiny velvet box from his shirt's pocket and opened it to reveal a plain silver ring. "I'm going to ask her to marry me," he said proudly.

"Are you insane?" Wayne exclaimed. "You're only seventeen, damn it!"

"So are you, *Wayne*."

"I'm not the one proposing to my pregnant girlfriend, *Dave*."

Returning the box to his pocket, David Brooks said, "Look, there's nothing you can say that will change my mind, okay? She's not getting an abortion and it's my responsibility to take good care of my kid. I am going to marry her and then we are moving to Dallas, that's it."

Wayne gave a loud sigh. "And leave me alone with Dean?"

"You'll be fine," David assured him.

"Dean is getting out of control, Dave. What if I can't find him any boys and he decides to target me? I won't be able to handle that torture rack, man."

David tightened his jaw. "I don't think you have any other options."

After thinking about this for quite some time, Wayne looked his friend in the eyes and said, "I'm going to run away."

"Where to?"

"None of your business."

"Come on, Wayne, it's not like I'm going to tell anyone."

Their food arrived and they ate in silence for a while, listening to the sounds of the buzzing mall in the background.

"Mount Pleasant," Wayne Henley finally said. "I have a cousin there who will be able to help me find a job." Biting into the burger, the smell of fresh pickles filled his nostrils. But when he chewed and swallowed, the sour taste of the burger got caught in the back of his throat.

"I've never been to Mount Pleasant," David said matter-of-factly. "Is it really that *pleasant*?"

"How should I know?" Wayne answered. "I haven't been there either. It's four and a half hours from here by car. On my motorcycle, more likely five."

They finished their meals fifteen minutes later and then David drove to his girlfriend's house to "pop the question." Wayne went to his mother's place to pack his bags for Mount Pleasant.

***

When David Brooks returned to Dean's apartment shortly after 4 p.m. Joseph Lyles was dead. His body was already covered in plastic sheeting and tied with ropes and duct tape.

"You found one by yourself?" David said upon seeing the "package" on the floor. The head was strapped so heavily with tape that he couldn't make out the face.

"Yeah," Dean replied, "but I couldn't have any fun with this one. The punk bit me." He held up his left hand, where blood was seeping through the teeth marks between his thumb and index finger.

"The scumbag!" David played along. "What was his name?"

"I'll tell you all about it later," said Dean. "I have taken a polaroid picture of him. But first we need to go put him away."

"In the boat shed?"

Dean shook his head slowly. "No, this one doesn't deserve to be buried in the shed. He's going to Jefferson County Beach."

David kept quiet. He could see Dean wasn't in the mood for an argument.

"Where is Wayne?" Dean asked as they bent down simultaneously to pick up the corpse.

"I don't know," David lied.

CHAPTER 23

JUNE 1973

Wayne couldn't keep a job in Mount Pleasant (which wasn't so pleasant after all, he had found out) so he returned to Houston in the summer of 1973.

By then, Dean had moved again, this time to his father's three-bedroomed bungalow at 2020 Lamar Drive in Pasadena. Recovering from a heavy flu and a hydrocele, he was too weak to scold Wayne for running away and, besides, Wayne had brought a friend along.

"Dean, this is Billy-Ray Lawrence," Wayne said when he arrived at the bungalow on the evening of June 4th. "Billy, this is Dean Corll."

Dean was in his element, despite his sore body. While Wayne had been away, David hadn't brought him any boys whatsoever. He was too busy pampering his pregnant fiancée. She wasn't really showing yet, so the couple had decided to wait with the marriage until the last minute.

Fifteen-year-old Billy-Ray greeted Dean, then walked into the bungalow, saying, "Wow, this is such a cozy little house." He had a slender body and his long black hair was tucked behind his elf-like ears. Wayne had told him there was going to be a wild party at this place tonight.

"Are you staying over?" Dean asked. It was a Monday and he was still on sick leave until that Friday. Plenty of time to play with young Billy-Ray Lawrence.

Billy untucked the shirt of his boy scout uniform and then looked at Wayne for approval. "I don't know, should I?"

"We're going fishing tomorrow, at Lake Sam Rayburn," Dean lied. "Do you want to come with?"

"I will have to phone my dad first," the boy answered.

Dean showed him where the telephone was, in the corridor leading from the lounge to the bedrooms, and then listened as Billy-Ray told his father that he was going on a fishing trip with "some friends."

When he hung up, Dean gave him a short tour of the house. There were five doors in the corridor. The two to the right led into a bathroom (decorated with ugly wallpaper) and the main bedroom (the only room in the house with an air conditioning unit). The doors to the left led into two smaller bedrooms containing very little furniture and mattresses on the floors. Behind the fifth door, at the end of the passageway, was a kitchen that seemed out of place, almost as if it had been added after the main structure had been built. The kitchen had high ceilings with build-in wooden cupboards, a gas stove-oven combination under a bay window, and a tall refrigerator in one corner. The ceramic floor tiles here were black and white squares, reminding Billy-Ray of a giant chess board.

In the meanwhile, Wayne had poured drinks on a booze cabinet on the other side of the house – double vodkas mixed with 7-Up – and tuned the radio to a station playing rock music.

Dean and Billy joined him in the lounge after the house tour and Dean handed each of the teenagers two LSD capsules, which they drank without hesitation.

"So, do you go to school?" Dean asked when they took their seats, across from Wayne.

Billy-Ray shook his head. "Nope. I dropped out at the end of last year. I now help my dad sort letters. He works in the mailroom at the Houston Post."

"I see," Dean replied, blinking his eyes. "And your mom? What does she do for a living?"

"She looks after the house and things like that."

"And they're okay with you just doing what you feel like in the evenings?" Dean wanted to know.

"Pretty much," said Billy-Ray. He finished his vodka and turned to Wayne, holding the glass upside down. "This is good stuff right here. Is there more?"

"Of course," Wayne replied. His glass was also empty. He took the glass from Billy and walked to the cabinet to refill for the two of them. Dean had barely touched his drink up to this point.

Twenty minutes later, the LSD kicked in, together with the alcohol, and Wayne Henley was the first to collapse. He was still talking about the latest Pink Floyd album, *The Dark Side of the Moon*, when his head suddenly fell to the side, onto his left shoulder, and he started snoring.

"What's wrong with him?" Billy-Ray slurred. His eyes were hazy and he was struggling to keep them open, Dean noticed. Before he could respond to the silly question, the boy slumped forward and ended up face down on the carpet, unconscious.

***

The next morning, Billy-Ray Lawrence awoke to find himself tied to the bed in the main bedroom, flat on his stomach. His clothes were gone, his mouth was dry and the thick hemp ropes were cutting into his bare wrists and ankles. Looking around, he saw that the door was closed and that all the curtains in the room were drawn. It was hot and humid and he didn't know what time it was.

"Hello!" he called out. "Is anybody there?"

Silence.

Wriggling around in a panic, Billy tried to free himself but the more he moved, the more the ropes hurt him. He could smell urine and when he lifted his pelvis slightly and lowered it down onto the bedsheet again, he realized he had wet himself.

"Hello!" he called again. "Dean! Wayne! Anybody!"

When there still came no answer, he began to cry loudly.

***

Dean Corll had spent the day driving to Lake Sam Rayburn and back, and he only returned to the bungalow in Pasadena late on the afternoon of June 5th. By then, Billy-Ray had been alone in the bedroom for seven hours and he was going out of his mind. He was dehydrated and weak to a point where he could barely speak.

He turned his head slightly when the bedroom door suddenly opened. "Dean," he murmured, "Why did you tie me up? I am in pain and I'm thirsty." Then his head dropped back onto the smelly bed and he started crying again.

After assisting his captive in drinking a glass of water, Dean spoke in a cynical tone: "Naughty, needy Billy-Ray. Look at you, all tied up and begging. I guess the next thing you're going to tell me is that you are hungry, isn't it?"

The boy didn't reply.

Dean placed an aluminium toolbox he was carrying on the floor, then sat down on a dry corner of the bed and said, "Are you left-handed or right-handed?"

"Right-handed," Billy-Ray whimpered.

"All right, I'm going to untie your right hand now," Dean told him. "After you have performed a simple task for me, I will let you go."

He freed Billy's right hand and then produced a postcard, a pen and a sheet of paper from his toolbox. "I want you to copy everything that I've written on this piece of paper exactly like that onto the postcard, do you understand?"

Billy-Ray nodded, wiping tears from his cheeks with the back of his hand.

"Don't try to do anything stupid now," said Dean. He placed the blank postcard and the sheet of paper on the bed in front of the teenager. "I assume you know all about postcards with your daddy working in the in the Houston Post mailroom and all that."

Taking the pen from the older man, Billy-Ray wrote the words down with trembling fingers:

Dear Daddy,

I have decided to go to Austin because I have got a good job offer. I am sorry that I decided to leave but I just had to go.

I will be back in late August. Hope you understand, but I had to go.

Daddy I hope you know I love you.

Your son,

Billy-Ray.

"Good boy," Dean said when he was finished. He picked up the postcard, jerked the pen from Billy's hand and then proceeded to tie the boy's hand to the bedpost once more.

"Wait!" Billy said in a blind panic. "You said you were going to release me!"

Dean sneered. "I lied, you dumbass."

CHAPTER 24

JUNE 1973

Billy-Ray Lawrence was kept alive for three excruciating days.

During this time, Dean tortured him with tools from his toolbox and raped him on several occasions. He didn't give the youth any food and only provided him with two glasses of water per day.

By night three, Wayne Henley returned from another trip to Dallas.

"Why are you still keeping him alive?" he asked Dean. "It's getting smelly in that room, you know?"

"Because I like him, Wayne. He's been a lot of fun, but you're right: it is time to let go."

"When are you going to kill him?"

"Tonight," Dean replied. "I had a telephone conversation with my mother this afternoon and she informed me that my stepfather is flying to Europe early tomorrow morning. That means he will not be able to visit his log cabin at Lake Sam Rayburn. I still have a key to the place, so we're going fishing and we'll get rid of the body while we are there."

Just then, David Brooks walked into the house.

"Ah, the groom to be," Dean said sarcastically. "What are you doing here? Aren't you supposed to be with your fiancée somewhere?"

"I spoke to Wayne on the phone and he said you had a boy here," David clarified. "Where is he?"

Dean waved a dismissive hand. "In my room. Go check for yourself."

It was already after eleven o'clock in the evening and David was dead-tired. After he had looked at the battered and bruised Billy-Ray in Dean's bedroom, he fell asleep in the opposite room, his skin crawling with repugnance.

He woke up the following morning and learned that Wayne and Dean had strangled the boy to death during the night and that they had already placed the body in the wooden box. He was relieved; he couldn't stomach the way Billy had been tortured. It had given him nightmares.

He helped Wayne to load the box into Dean's white van and then they drove to Jake West's log cabin at Lake Sam Rayburn.

When they arrived at noon, Dean unlocked the cabin door and retrieved two fishing rods from the wardrobe in the living area. He gave the rods (and a can of worms he'd bought at Art's Angling Shop in Huntington) to David and Wayne and told them to go fishing; that he needed some time to think and scout for a location where they could bury the corpse.

"I can't believe he is so casual about getting rid of the body," David mentioned as they walked down to the lake shoreline, sweating. It was cloudy but warm and stuffy; one of those Texas days when people struggled to breathe.

"Dean's always been like that," Wayne replied, tapping his skull with two fingers. "Something's not right in his head." Like David, he was casually dressed in a t-shirt, shorts and a baseball cap.

Upon reaching the fishing pier Dean had showed them on a map, David Brooks removed his glasses and cleaned them with his shirt. "Why do you think he tortures the guys we bring him like that?" he asked Wayne. "I mean, I can understand his sexual desires, but why hurt them?"

"I think I know the reason why," Wayne replied, biting his fingernails. He carefully put the fishing rod down on the dilapidated pier and placed his hands on his hips. "One evening last year, when Dean was quite stoned, he told me about his year in the army. Apparently, there were some guys who found out that he was a homosexual and they beat him up badly for it. I think that might have scarred his emotions and now he takes it out on the boys we supply to him."

David didn't have anything to say to that. It sounded to him like a logical explanation for Dean Corll's sadistic and violent behaviour.

They fished for five hours – without catching anything – and then returned to the log cabin when the mosquitos were just about carrying them away down at the lake.

Arriving at the cabin, David and Wayne were stunned to find Dean cooking pork ribs on a portable barbeque on the porch, while whistling The Beatles' song, *Piggies*.

"What the hell, Dean?" David said, throwing his arms in the air. "There is a dead body in the van and you're making food? Fucking incredible!"

"Can't work on an empty belly," Dean replied, turning the ribs with a stainless steel pair of tongs. "Besides, it's not dark yet. People might see us." He looked up at David and added, "How about 'thank you for making us something to eat, Dean'? You know, you've been sponging on me for years and you never show any gratitude."

David ripped off his baseball cap and went inside to take a shower while Wayne lit a cigarette and joined Dean on the patio. "It actually makes sense," he said, waving a mosquito away with his hand. "I don't know why Dave went off like that."

"I take it you didn't catch anything?" Dean said absently.

Wayne dragged on his cigarette. "Nope. This lake is dead, I tell you." He pointed at Dean's van. "Just like old Billy-Ray over there."

After eating ribs and corn on the cob, they drove four miles north, to a spot Dean had chosen for the burial. Wayne kept lookout in the van while David and Dean dug the grave near a service dirt road, where the ground was moist but not as swampy as on the stretch between the cabin and the lake.

It was now after dark and the faint light of a half-moon was breaking through the clouds. There were less mosquitos here in the woods and Dean was relieved. The little creatures had really climbed into him back at Jake's cabin.

When the grave was deep enough, they removed the body from the wooden box and buried it. While Dean was covering the hole with soil, he said to David, "Go fetch the rug in the back of my van."

David frowned but did as he was told.

He returned with the grimy green rug over his shoulder and asked, "What is this for?"

Dean had now levelled the soil over the grave and he indicated a heap of dirt next to it. "To get rid of the extra dirt. Otherwise it will show a mound and anybody driving past will be able to see that we've buried something here."

They shovelled the excess dirt onto the rug and carried it to the lake where they dumped it into the seemingly black water.

"There, all done," Dean said, dusting off his hands. "Let's go back and get some sleep."

***

Less than two weeks later, they were back at the same spot with the corpse of a man by the name of Raymond Blackburn.

Blackburn, twenty years old and a builder by trade, had come to the city of Houston from Baton Rouge, Louisiana, to work on a large construction project in The Heights. Then he received news on Friday, June 15th, that his pretty wife had given birth to their very first child.

Raymond asked the construction foreman in Houston for the weekend off and hitchhiked back to Louisiana to see his new-born baby.

Standing at the intersection of Airline Drive and Cavalcade Street, with a five-o'clock shadow on his chin, the young man with his thumb in the air didn't have to wait long for an opportunity in an easterly direction.

The ride he received didn't take him anywhere near Louisiana, though. It first took him to 2020 Lamar Drive in Pasadena, where he was murdered by the madman, Dean Corll, and then to his shallow grave at Lake Sam Rayburn.

Raymond Blackburn never got the chance to see the face of his only child.

CHAPTER 25

JULY 1973

Wayne lured fifteen-year-old Homer Garcia to Dean's Lamar Drive lair next.

It was a warm Saturday evening, on July 7th, when he rode into the driveway on his motorcycle with Homer sitting on the seat behind him. Dean watched through the lounge window as the two teenagers climbed off the motorbike and made their way to the front door.

"Welcome to the best Independence Day party in town," he said upon opening the door. "You guys are a little early. I haven't prepared everything yet and David is still on the way with the fireworks."

"Dean, this is Homer," Wayne introduced the visitor. "I befriended him at the Coaches Driving School in Bellaire yesterday. He is from southwest Houston."

"Nice to meet you," Dean said, staring at Homer Garcia. The boy was muscled with prominent facial features and wavy raven-black hair. He reminded Dean of himself when he was younger.

Homer shook the older man's hand while saying, "Thanks for having me, but... but I really need to take a leak. I've been keeping it in for more than an hour now."

They quickly went inside and Wayne showed Homer where the bathroom was.

While the visitor was taking care of his business, Dean said to Wayne, "That's a good-looking boy right there, man. I want more of that kind." He removed his wallet from his pocket, took out two hundred dollar notes and handed it to Wayne. "Money well earned, my friend."

Wayne mumbled a "Thanks," then slid the cash into his pocket and went to the kitchen to fetch a six-pack of beer, a box of Cherry Toastette pastries and a bag of fresh Banana Flip Twinkies Dean had bought for their Independence Day party.

As soon as they had all settled down in the lounge and began to feast on the snacks, David Brooks arrived with the fireworks. Dean had given him three hundred dollars earlier that afternoon to spend on the customary midsummer entertaining pyrotechnics.

"Toys for boys!" he announced upon barging through the front door. He held up two large brown paper bags and the others stood up to inspect the contents. There were Volcano Rockets, Helicopter Crackers, Astrolites, Silver Rain Missiles and Olympic Torches, amongst others.

Homer was beside himself. "Oh my soul!" he yawped. "I've never seen these things from up close!" Coming from a poor family he had only seen fireworks from a distance, every year during the fourth of July celebrations at the AstroWorld amusement park in Houston, not far from his mother's house.

When he informed the others about this, Dean's face grew sombre and he asked, "Homer, does your mother know that you are here tonight?"

"No, she doesn't," he replied. "I told her that I'm spending the night at a friend's place but I didn't say who. Why, is there going to be some kind of a problem?"

Dean smiled. "Not at all. I just sort of like to keep my parties a secret from the parents, you know?" He placed an arm around Homer's shoulders and whispered, "I don't want to be accused of giving out free beer and weed to guys who are still in school, that's all. Now, what do you say we go outside and shoot some of those rockets?"

"Can I light one?" Homer asked excitedly.

"Hell, you can light them all!" Dean replied, slapping the youth on the back.

They went outside, onto the driveway, and the serial killing trio watched as Homer Garcia fired one rocket after the other into the night sky, a high-pitched shrieking sound escaping his mouth with each spectacular launch. He was thoroughly enjoying himself out there.

An hour later, all Dean's fireworks had been ignited and they stayed outside for a little while longer, looking at some of the other people's explosions, painting the atmosphere around the neighborhood in bright yellow, orange, silver, pink and blue.

"Man, that was fun!" Homer said once they were back inside the bungalow. "This is a party I will never, ever forget. Thank you, guys!"

Wayne passed around more beer and shared his marijuana joint with the visitor, while David and Dean were cranking up the stereo with the latest 70s hits from Elton John, Johnny Nash, Jackson Brown and Neil Young to name but a few.

At a stage late in the evening, Homer Garcia – now pretty drunk and completely spaced-out on doobie – fell down against Dean's wooden box in the corner of the lounge. "What's this crate for?" he asked while pushing himself back to his feet with unsteady arms.

"You're gonna like it a lot," Wayne told him. "Just wait and see, buddy." He walked down the corridor and returned moments later with two pairs of handcuffs.

Handing the cuffs to Homer, he lifted the lid of the box and then turned his back on the visitor. "First cuff my hands behind my back," he said, "then cuff my ankles together."

It took Homer a while to figure out how the handcuffs worked but he managed in the end. Once Wayne was properly manacled, he clumsily climbed into the box and asked Homer to close the lid.

When he emerged a free man, seconds later, Homer clapped his hands enthusiastically. "How on earth did you manage to do that?" he said with a flabbergasted expression on his face.

"Let me show you," Wayne replied, grinning.

***

Forty minutes later, Homer Garcia was in tremendous pain and begging for his life.

He was standing in the same bathroom he had used when he first entered the house and blood was streaming from his chest. Dean had shot him at close range, through his right lung, and his breathing was now a hoarse gargle. "Please don't kill me!" he rasped, clutching his cuffed hands over the gaping bullet wound. "I need a doctor!"

The pain from inside of him completely dulled the other bruises, all over his body, where Dean and Wayne had repeatedly struck him with various blunt objects for half an hour. He couldn't understand why they had done it. They were so friendly before; now they were like monsters.

Looking up from his chest, he watched as Dean Corll raised the pistol for a second time and aimed it at his head. Wayne Henley was standing behind the sadistic thirty-three-year-old man, urging him to "finish him off, man."

"Please!" Homer yelled, sounding like a boy with a severe case of asthma.

Then Dean pulled the trigger and shot him in the forehead.

Homer Garcia fell backward, into the bathtub, and died within seconds. The fireworks night he'd said he would never forget had come to a tragic end.

His body was left to bleed out in the tub before it was taken to Lake Sam Rayburn, where Dean buried it not too far from the corpses of Raymond Blackburn and Billy-Ray Lawrence.

CHAPTER 26

JULY 1973

The parents in Houston were beginning to accuse the local police department of incompetence.

While the Chief of Police kept on saying that the tallying number of missing boys merely represented another wave of "runaways", the parents believed otherwise. There were just too many boys going missing in such a short space of time. Furthermore, many parents had logical explanations as to why their sons wouldn't have left home on impulse: "Wally did not even take his bicycle…" "Billy left without saying goodbye and that's just not like him…" "Why would Ruben leave forty dollars in his room and then run away? It doesn't make sense."

Some of these missing boys were school dropouts and some not. Some came from broken families and some not. There was no distinct pattern, barring the fact that most of them were between thirteen and eighteen years old, the police argued. They just didn't know where to start to look, so they told the parents that their hands were tied.

Nevertheless, the members of the community were deeply concerned.

So was Dean Corll.

He was busy watching the evening news on a black-and-white television in Jake West's cabin at Lake Sam Rayburn, when one of the parents said to a reporter: "We should stand together and actively search for our missing sons. I believe that they were abducted and I am urging all the other parents to come up with a detailed description of the clothes their sons were wearing on the day they went missing. If we can find even one piece of clothing, we could track down the perpetrators."

Did you cover your tracks properly? Dean thought, sipping on a cold beer. *Did you make sure to get rid of all the clothing, you son of a bitch*? His mind told him yes, but he had murdered so many boys that he couldn't keep track anymore.

"Let's do this by location," he now said aloud, starting to count on his fingers.

He recalled that the bodies he'd buried at High Island Beach had all been naked, but he had burned their clothes. The ones in the boat shed had mostly been naked as well; all their clothes were in plastic bags, safely locked away in the shed. Joseph Lyles, the one who had bitten him, had still been fully dressed when he'd gone into the ground at Jefferson County Beach. And the ones he had buried here at Lake Sam Rayburn? Well, their clothes were in a box at his bungalow in Lamar Drive.

Satisfied with his recollection of the events, Dean got up and went outside where David and Wayne were playing cards around a pine table on the porch. It was still early in the evening and the blazing sun was just about to go down in the dry and dusty west.

"Let's take a drive around the lake," Dean instructed. "I need another boy."

Because it was so windy outside, the two teenagers agreed to the plan. The hot and swirling breeze was blowing the cards off the table every few seconds and it was disruptive to their game.

They had come to the log cabin on Wayne Henley's request; he had grown fond of the place ever since the first time Dean had brought him and David here. Jake West was away on a candy festival in New York City, so he didn't know about the uninvited visitors on his holiday property.

Dean drove south until they reached a bridge with a large white sign reading: NO FISHING FROM BRIDGE. Right underneath the signboard sat two men with fishing rods in their hands, angling away merrily in the dusky light.

"Such a disregard for the rules," Dean mumbled.

"Says you," David shot back.

"Shut up," Dean told him. "Open your eyes and scout, will you?"

About two miles beyond the bridge there was an old blue car standing in a patch of sand on the side of the road. The badge and name was gone from the rear of the vehicle, but the trio agreed that it was a Chevy, based on the shape and the amount of chrome strips covering the fenders and doors.

Dean parked his van behind the blue car, twenty yards before the strip of sand, and David climbed out to approach the abandoned vehicle.

Moments later, a teenager the same age as Wayne and David emerged from the bushes next to the van and started speaking to David.

Rolling down the van's window, Dean called, "What seems to be the matter?"

"This is John Sellars," David replied. "His car is stuck in the sand over there. He asked if we could give him a ride to Huntington."

Dean gave a bright smile. "Of course we can."

Young John Sellers took off his cowboy hat and clutched it in both hands. "Thank you," he said in a humble tone of voice. "Thank you so much. Just give me a second." He quickly gathered his backpack from his car's trunk and then returned for the promised ride.

Once he was in the back of the van, Dean drove off while asking, "Where are you from?"

"Orange County," John replied.

Wayne turned to face the stranger. "Damn, that's a long way from here. California, huh?"

"No, stupid," David said, chuckling. "Texas."

Turning his head back to the front, Wayne blushed. "How was I supposed to know there is an Orange County in Texas?"

"Well, there is," Dean confirmed. He stepped on the accelerator and took a detour to Huntington, to go past the location where they had buried Billy-Ray Lawrence, Raymond Blackburn and Homer Garcia over the past six weeks.

"What are you guys shooting?" John Sellars asked from the back, pointing at a hunting rifle mounted against the van's back door.

"Ducks," David said, "but we haven't shot one yet. We only arrived this afternoon."

"We'll probably go out early tomorrow morning," Wayne added. Then he took his harmonica out of his shirt's pocket and began to play random tunes.

When they reached the spot where they had buried the three bodies, Dean stopped the van and then his face turned ashen. He spoke in a low voice when he said, "Shit. I think there is something sticking out."

David and Wayne stared through the windshield, where the Ford's headlights were casting a tunnel of white light ahead of them. The clear outline of a human foot was protruding from the moist brown soil beside the gravel road. John Sellars didn't see any of this; he wasn't paying attention. He was busy rummaging through his backpack, in search of his wallet.

"I'll take care of it," David said, opening the passenger door. After getting out, he scanned the surroundings for any movement or sounds and then approached the jutting foot.

Wayne was still playing his harmonica and Dean never heard the back door being opened from the inside. The next time he looked up from the dashboard, Sellars was standing right behind David with his hand over his mouth. David was still covering the shallow grave with gravel and John Sellars must have seen the corpse's foot, Dean realized.

He jumped out, ran to the back of the van and grabbed his hunting rifle. Then he turned to the spectacle and said, "David, get out of the way," while lifting the rifle into a horizontal position.

Before John Sellers could gather his thoughts, David fell down onto his stomach and Dean fired four bullets into John's chest. His body made a loud thump as it hit the ground a second later.

"He saw what you were doing," Dean told David, who raised his eyes and looked intensely at the dead body, inches away from his outstretched arms.

Dean picked up the empty rifle shells and then hauled John's body to the van, with Wayne's assistance, while David finished up the repair job on the grave.

"We cannot bury him here," Dean said to Wayne as they placed the corpse on the dirty rug in the back of the van. "Someone might have heard the shots. We'd better get out of here soon."

They made a brief stop at the cabin – to pack their bags and remove any evidence that someone had been there – and then drove back to the location where John's car was standing on the side of the road. It was now pitch dark with no sign of a moon anywhere in the night sky.

Using some of the ropes Dean always kept in his van, they managed to pull the Chevy from the sand with the Ford Econoline. Then they drove John's car out of sight, into a wooded area four miles further east and set the car alight with a gallon of fuel and a disposable lighter.

After that, Dean drove to his original graveyard, High Island Beach, where the corpse was buried shortly before midnight on July 12th 1973, two days before John Sellars would have turned eighteen.

CHAPTER 27

JULY 1973

The intensity and frequency of Dean Corll's killing spree now began to increase rapidly.

Exactly one week after the death of John Sellars, he and Wayne murdered Tony Baulch, a fifteen-year-old boy from Houston Heights. David wasn't with them this time – he was on honeymoon in New Orleans with his pregnant wife. They had tied the knot the previous weekend.

The Baulch family had already lost Tony's older brother, Billy, whom Wayne had strangulated a year earlier. They still regarded him as missing and were still looking for him when his younger sibling disappeared on July 19th. Tony Baulch was on his way to get a haircut at the same barber shop where his brother and Johnny Delome had been abducted, when Wayne promised him some money and free beer if he took a ride with him and Dean in the white van.

Four hours later, after Dean had repeatedly raped and beaten him, Tony Baulch was choked to death with a *Houston Lighting and Power* electrical cable and buried at Lake Sam Rayburn the following night.

This was the twenty-fifth victim since it had all started in the fall of 1970.

***

Less than a week after Tony's burial, Wayne Henley was in for yet another payment of four hundred dollars.

He was driving along West 27th Street when he spotted two youths sitting on the lush green lawn in front of a house for sale, sharing a marijuana joint in the shade of a Live Oak tree. It was another hot afternoon and both boys had taken off their shirts and tied them around their waists.

When Wayne got out of the van, he instantly recognized one of them as Charles Cobble, a brown-haired guy with a tanned skin who had been in his class in seventh grade. The other one was pale in comparison, and his blond hair was combed to the side. Wayne hadn't seen him before.

"Hey, Charlie," he said as he approached the lawn, "who's your friend?"

"Hello, Wayne," Charles replied, standing up. "This is Marty Jones. He is now living with me."

Wayne frowned. "Living with you? How's Deb taking it?" He knew that Charles Cobble was in a similar position to the one David Brooks was in. He had made his girlfriend, Deborah, pregnant and had been forced to marry her by his parents, at age seventeen."

Charles pulled Marty up with one hand and then shrugged. "Well, we kind of separated, you know?"

"Too bad," Wayne replied, also shrugging his shoulders. He shook Marty's hand. "Hi, I'm Wayne Henley, nice to meet you."

Marty mumbled back something inaudible and then Charles said, glancing at the white van in the street, "Nice wheels, man. I've never seen you in that bad boy before."

"It's not mine," Wayne clarified. "It belongs to this super cool dude, Dean Corll. There is always a party at his house and there's never a shortage of beer and doobie."

"Oh yeah, I know of him!" Marty said. "He was called the Candy Man when we were still in elementary school. I remember because I always used to go and play pool at his mom's candy factory across the road from Helms."

Wayne nodded, then shifted his attention back to Charles Cobble. "Listen, Charlie, what are you guys doing tonight?"

"We haven't planned anything," Cobble answered. "Probably just gonna watch TV and stuff."

"Why don't you come with me to Dean's place?" Wayne suggested, pointing at the joint in Marty's left hand. "There's plenty more of *that* and a shitload of beer."

Charles and Marty didn't hesitate at all. They simply couldn't say no to a party where there was going to be free beer and marijuana.

Once they were inside the van with Wayne Henley, both still shirtless and sweating in the pulsing heat, Charles asked, "How's Dave Brooks doing?"

"He'll be alright," Wayne replied. "Got married last week. His wife looks like she's swallowed two soccer balls, though."

That brought out a fit of laughter from Marty Jones.

They arrived at 2020 Lamar Drive a little over half an hour later and Dean Corll didn't waste any time whatsoever. After Wayne had introduced the new visitors to him, he handed out cans of beer, poured himself a strong bourbon in a tumbler glass and then asked Wayne to show the newcomers the handcuff trick. Loud rock music was blaring from the stereo on the liquor cabinet.

Charles and Marty were just about finished with their beers when Wayne performed his magic trick, then cuffed them and told them he had lost the keys.

"They both look pretty strong, Wayne," Dean said, grimacing. "Let's find out who the better fighter is, shall we?"

They dragged the kidnapped youths into the main bedroom where Wayne held them down while Dean first uncuffed their hands and feet, and then re-cuffed only their left wrists and left ankles to opposite sides of the torture board against the wall.

"Now punch Charlie in the face," Dean told Marty.

Instead of obeying the order, Marty Jones started screaming for help. Charles joined him soon, yelling even harder.

Wayne swiftly taped their mouths shut with the ever-present roll of black duct tape on the bedside table. Dean retrieved his rubber whip from the built-in wardrobe and started beating them, the cracking sounds echoing in the sparsely furnished room.

"If you hit one another he will stop!" Wayne shouted over the noise of the whip tearing into human flesh.

This time the teenagers listened. They began to punch and kick each other relentlessly, both with tears now streaming down their cheeks.

"Good," Dean said. He stopped wielding the whip and sat down on the side of the bed. "Let me make you a deal: the first one to knock the other one unconscious, I will let go."

Charles and Marty kept on fighting for another five to six minutes, then they became tired and their limbs stopped moving.

Dean stood up from the bed and took off his clothes without speaking.

Wayne Henley smoked three cigarettes as he watched how Dean sexually assaulted Charles Cobble for quite some time before finally returning to the bed, breathing heavily.

"Now shoot the fucker," Dean told Wayne.

Picking up Dean's pistol from a chest of drawers in the corner, Wayne slowly lifted it and then shot Charles twice in the back of his head. Blood and brain matter exploded into the humid air and Charles Cobble's body instantly went limp on the torture board. Marty Jones was shaking his head violently, trying to scream through the duct tape.

"The other one too!" Dean Corll barked.

Wayne pulled the trigger again, but this time the gun only made a faint clicking sound.

"It's out of bullets," he said in a hushed voice.

That was when Dean recalled what he had forgotten to buy the previous day: cartridges. He had gone into town to buy new venetian blinds for his bedroom and bullets for his pistol, but the latter had somehow slipped his mind. The blinds were still in the box on the bedroom's carpet and he now opened it to take out one of the cords designed to manoeuvre the blinds around.

Within a flash, he was onto Marty Jones and strangled him to death in under two minutes.

While they were preparing the corpses with lime powder and plastic sheeting, Wayne asked, "Are we taking them to the lake?"

"Nope," replied Dean. "I did some cleaning up last night, so there is now more space in the front of my boat shed. These troopers are going to Silver Bell Street."

CHAPTER 28

AUGUST 1973

On August 3rd 1973, Dean Corll killed his last victim, although he didn't know it at the time.

Thirteen-year-old James Dreymala walked out into the backyard of their house in Pasadena – where his mother was taking down the laundry from the washing line – early on that quiet Friday evening. It wasn't dark yet, but the twilight was briskly turning from pinkish-red to a deep purple-black.

He was rather excited, since he was planning on taking his girlfriend to see the new James Bond movie, *Live and let Die*, that coming Sunday afternoon. Everybody in town was buzzing about the film, because the much younger British actor, Roger Moore, was taking over the role of James Bond from the retiring Sean Connery for the first time.

James nearly had enough money to pay for the tickets for him and his girlfriend; he only had to make one last stop on his red bicycle, then he would be sorted. He never received any pocket money from his penniless parents and the way he generated his income was to mow lawns and return empty soda bottles to the grocery store in order to collect the deposits.

"Mama," he said out in the yard, "I'm just going down to the store to exchange some empties, okay?"

His mother peeked from behind a clean bedsheet on the line and frowned. "Why now?"

"I need to get the money to pay for my movie date on Sunday," James replied.

"Can't you go tomorrow?"

"They don't accept empties on Saturdays, Mama. They are too busy."

Mrs Dreymala sighed. "You know I don't want you out riding your bike after dark, Jimmy."

James clasped his hands together with a smack. "I'll be back in just a few moments. I'm not going to be long, I promise."

"All right, all right," his mother said, dragging the words out in her heavy Texas accent.

James Dreymala dashed back into the house to grab his rucksack full of clanging soda bottles and was out in the street on his bicycle thirty seconds later.

Six blocks further, as the grocery store's front window was coming into view, a white van drove past him and then stopped in front of him, blocking his way. He was just about to go onto the sidewalk when an older boy with eyeglasses climbed out the van and greeted him.

"Hi there, young man," he said. "My name is Dave Brooks. What are you doing alone out in the streets after dark?"

"None of your business," James told him, turning the bicycle's steering wheel to the right.

The empty glass bottles in his rucksack made a clanking noise as he eased the bike into motion and then David said, "Ah, you're returning empties, right? Well, in that case I have a surprise for you."

This made James Dreymala's ears twitch. He'd always been an inquisitive boy and whenever the word "surprize" came up, he simply *had* to know wat it was. He stopped the bicycle again, stared at the older boy and asked, "What is it?"

"See this van?" David Brooks said, touching the Ford's rear door. "The man it belongs to is one of my close friends and he has a whole garage full of empty Coke bottles. Just the other day, he was complaining about how he doesn't have the energy to take them all to the store."

"Wow," James replied with wide eyes. "You think he would let me take them?"

"I know he will..." David's words trailed off, in search of a name.

"Jimmy," said James Dreymala. "You can call me Jimmy."

"Well, Jimmy, why don't you go down to the store really quickly and return those bottles in your backpack. I will wait here and then we'll take you to the house with all the Coca Cola empties. It's not too far from here."

David watched as James pedalled to the grocery store, thinking about the two hundred dollars he was about to earn. He was back with Dean and Wayne for the night, while his wife was recovering from giving birth in one of Houston's public hospitals.

Inside the store, James exchanged his bottles for three dollars and then asked the store clerk if he could use the telephone on the counter.

Dialling his home number, he waited until his father picked up.

"Daddy," he said, "will you please tell Mama that I am running a little late. I just need to make one more stop before I come home."

"You listen to me, James Dreymala," his father warned in a firm voice. "You get your butt back to the house NOW, do you hear me? You are not too old for a hiding."

Glancing at a large clock against the grocery store's stone wall, James said, "Okay, Daddy, I'll be back home in twenty minutes."

***

Twenty minutes later, he was nowhere near his home.

He was on the torture board in Dean's bedroom, the life being strangled from his fragile body with a nylon cord. Like many of the other victims, he had been molested and assaulted before his untimely death.

Young James Dreymala would never again mow a lawn or exchange an empty soda bottle for small change.

His life was over.

PART IV
ENDGAME

CHAPTER 29

Rhonda Williams was barely eighteen months old when her mother had passed away back in 1958; too young to remember the event in a lot of detail later in her life.

Now, fifteen years on, she was looking at a black-and-white photograph – taken on the day her mother had died – while standing in her bedroom, waiting for Wayne Henley to come fetch her. This photo, together with what her father (the lowlife) had told her, brought back some of the memories.

In the photograph was Catherine Fern Williams, sitting with her baby daughter, Rhonda, on her lap. Beside them stood Rhonda's two older sisters, both still toddlers, and her teenage brother who'd suffered from a mental condition that had caused his brain to stop developing at the tender age of ten. The mother and the three sisters were all wearing pretty white summer dresses and Rhonda's brother was dressed in khaki trousers and a chequered shirt.

The photo had been taken by Rhonda's grandmother who'd lived in Brownwood, about two hundred miles northwest of Houston.

"Mommy, how long until we get back to the farm?" one of Rhonda's sisters had asked once they'd said goodbye to Nana and were all crammed into her father's pickup truck, on their way home. Their father,

Ben Williams, had owned a large potato farm just outside of Houston back then.

"About four hours, pumpkin," her mother had answered with a smile.

When they'd arrived at the farmhouse late that afternoon, they had all gotten out of the pickup, except for Ben who had told them he was going into town to pick up a few groceries.

The four siblings had headed straight for the barn, where their two favorite cows *Sirloin* and *T-bone* were munching on alfalfa hay.

When they returned to the house twenty minutes later, their mother was dead on the porch.

A thoracic aortic aneurysm, the coroner announced the next day.

***

When Rhonda was just six years old, she tried to join her mother in the afterlife on one occasion.

Because she was the youngest child, she'd been assigned the smallest room in the farmhouse. It wasn't exactly a bedroom, but rather the old kitchen (her father had built a new one in the summer of 1961) and her bed was right next to a black gas stove, still in working condition.

When she returned home from school one afternoon, she fetched a Styrofoam cup from the kitchen and went into her "room" where she attached the cup to her nose and mouth with a rubber band she'd found in her schoolbag. Then she made a little hole in the bottom of the cup, pulled the gas pipe from the base of the stove and connected it to the cup.

The moment she sat down on the wooden floor and turned on the gas, her father stormed into the room, shouting, "What the hell are you doing?"

Rhonda began to sob, her shoulders quivering with fear and confusion. "I'm sorry, Daddy," she snivelled. "I cannot take it anymore. My sisters are just so mean to me."

"What are you talking about?" Ben Williams asked, crouching down beside her.

"They always tell me that it was my fault that Mommy died. They say if I was never born, she would still be alive."

"Well, that is simply not true, Rhonda," her father said. "I've explained it to you before: Mommy died from an aneurysm."

Little Rhonda was still too young to know who to believe, her father or her sisters. It was only many years later when she finally made peace with the fact that her mother's death hadn't been her fault.

A month after her seventh birthday, her father sold the farm and moved into town with Rhonda and her three siblings. Agriculture was dying in Texas and it was time for him to start a new business.

The big house on 23rd street had five bedrooms, so every child got their own room and that was quite nice, Rhonda thought at the time. There were many other kids in Houston Heights and she enjoyed making new friends. At the farm it had always only been her sisters and her brother and she was tired of them. Now, she was happy for the first time in her life.

However, that feeling didn't last very long.

A couple of months later, Ben's new girlfriend moved in and all four children soon agreed that she was a worse stepmother than Cinderella's.

She would scream and yell at Rhonda and her sisters all day and she would give them vicious hidings for the simplest of mistakes. Due to Rhonda's strong personality and her determination to fight back, she became the black sheep in no time.

It was during these years that Rhonda met Wayne Henley. He was a good-looking boy in her school – two years older than her – and she had a huge crush on him. His mother's house was only three houses from her father's, on the same street. Unfortunately for Rhonda, the older boys didn't want to be seen around younger girls, so she befriended one of Wayne's brothers – who was in the same grade she was in – with the hope of getting to know the older sibling better.

***

A few weeks before her twelfth birthday, Rhonda overheard a conversation between her father (who was now drinking strong spirits every night) and her stepmother. They were shouting in the kitchen while the children were watching television in the living room.

"Ben, you listen to me now. I want that little bitch out of here!"

"I agree that she's a handful sometimes," Rhonda's father slurred, "but where do you want me to send her to?"

"She can go to Solid Rock for all I care!" her stepmother yelled. "But I'm telling you, she is not my responsibility anymore. She has to go! It's either her or me."

Then Rhonda and her siblings heard their father make a telephone call from the dining room, but his voice was too faint to recognize anything he was saying.

Not too long after he'd hung up, Ben Williams staggered into the living room and told his youngest daughter: "Rhonda, pack your bags. You're leaving for Solid Rock tomorrow."

Rhonda was devastated.

Solid Rock Refuge for Girls was the one place every female child in Houston feared. From what Rhonda had heard, the place was just a few invisible flames short of hell.

The following morning, she was standing in the driveway, waiting for a taxi, when Wayne Henley rode by on his bicycle.

He stopped upon seeing her with the two suitcases in her hands and asked, "What's going on, girl?"

"They're sending me off to The Rock," Rhonda answered with a shiver in her voice. "Will you please tell my friends at school that I'm going to miss them?"

Wayne first nodded, then shook his head slowly. "Gee, Rhonda, that's bad, girl."

***

Solid Rock turned out to be as tough as rumours had it.

The head matron was a stern woman who didn't have any patience with ill-discipline. During the day, the girls had to slave away at cleaning, cooking, gardening and knitting. At night, they were locked in their rooms to prevent them from running off.

Rhonda Williams saved up her weekly allowance until she had enough money to buy a new padlock, similar to the one on her room's door. She gave the cash to Wayne, who bought the lock and secretly replaced the old one while he was there on one of his Sunday afternoon visits.

That night, Rhonda and her roommate escaped The Rock to hitchhike to California.

But they only made it to Brenham, halfway from Houston to Austin, where the police tracked them down in an abandoned house. When they were taken back to Solid Rock, the head matron said that Rhonda was "too much of a trouble maker" and threw her out.

After living briefly with her grandmother in Brownwood, Rhonda was enrolled in the Houston foster care system at age thirteen.

She was placed at a foster home within a month and started working as a waitress at the *Long John Silver* restaurant. That was where she met Frank Aguirre. They first became good friends and then started dating. Rhonda had now grown into an attractive teenage girl with curly chestnut hair and a bubbly personality; she was becoming a popular girl in Houston Heights.

On a cool evening in March 1972, Rhonda wasn't working and Frank called her from the restaurant to tell her he would swing by her house after his shift.

Rhonda waited until after midnight but he never came.

When she went to Frank's house the next day, his parents told her that he'd gone missing. She couldn't believe it. She couldn't understand how her first love could just pack up and go. Her friends said that Frank had probably found himself another girlfriend and disappeared with her.

Wayne Henley, on the other hand, lied to Rhonda and told her that he believed the Mafia had taken Frank. He did this with a straight face, knowing full well that Dean Corll had murdered Rhonda's boyfriend by strangling him to death with a nylon cord.

Not aware of his dark secret, Rhonda confided in seventeen-year-old Wayne and, before long, he became like an older brother to her.

CHAPTER 30

Early in 1973, Rhonda Williams – now fifteen – was walking to the park with Wayne's younger brother and a friend, Johnny Reyna, when Johnny lit a marijuana joint and passed it on to her.

As soon as she brought the joint to her lips, Wayne's brother shouted, "Cops!"

Rhonda looked up to see a police car coming around the corner. Thinking fast, she pushed the joint into her mouth and swallowed it whole. But the police officer had already seen her smoking, so she was put on probation, then removed from the foster home and returned to her father's house. He had broken up with his girlfriend by that stage, so she thought it would be safe and comfortable to live under the same roof as her dad once more.

She was wrong.

Ben Williams was now a complete alcoholic, and not one of those who turned friendly and loving when he got drunk. He became mean and violent. Rhonda cried herself to sleep on many a night, after receiving a brutal beating from her father. The other siblings had left the house and since it was only her and her father, he did pretty much whatever he liked to her. There was nobody to protect her.

One of the conditions of Rhonda's probation was that she had to see a psychologist once a week.

She asked Wayne Henley to accompany her to her first visit and, after that, it became a habit for the two of them to ride to the shrink's office together on their bicycles every Saturday morning. While she went in for her half-hour sessions, Wayne would wait outside and smoke Marlboros in the park.

After her second visit, Rhonda told the psychologist about her father's behaviour, saying that he abused her because he didn't want her and didn't love her. She was rather shocked with the shrink's response when he said, "Rhonda, what you need to do is go home and cook dinner and clean the house, then your dad will love you."

During this same time period, Wayne Henley was beginning to feel guilty about his part in all the boys he and Dean had murdered. He hadn't told anybody about it and he was now thinking of turning himself in to the police.

"Do you think the guy would talk to me?" he asked Rhonda when she came out of her psychology session one day.

"What guy?" Rhonda said, frowning.

Wayne stared uncomfortably at the ground. "You know, the shrink guy." He was feeling particularly overwhelmed on that specific day. It was August 4th and he had assisted Dean Corll in burying James Dreymala, his last victim, the previous night.

"Why would you want to talk to *him*?" Rhonda replied incredulously.

"Just some stuff I want to get off my chest, that's all."

Rhonda raised her bushy eyebrows. "What stuff? Why can't you talk to me?"

"Because it's boy's stuff," Wayne said. "Look, forget it, okay? Let's just go already."

"No, wait," Rhonda told him. "I'm sorry. Let me go and ask him. I'll be just a minute." She ran up the stairs and Wayne waited outside, holding their bicycles.

Returning a while later, with an angry look on her face, Rhonda said, "Unbelievable!" while taking her bicycle from Wayne and straddling it.

"What did he have to say?" Wayne asked.

Rhonda made a snorting sound. "Not only did he refuse to see you, he told me that my sessions are now over too, that I am wasting his time."

"Asshole," Wayne mumbled, also getting onto his bike.

They rode in silence for five blocks until Rhonda suddenly said, "Oh, no." She stopped her bicycle on the sidewalk and climbed off.

Wayne came to a halt next to her and looked at her bicycle's front wheel. "Flat tyre?"

"Yeah," Rhonda replied, sighing. "Isn't that just great?"

They walked their bicycles down Heights Boulevard, keeping in the cool shade of the row of Live Oak trees to their right. It was another scorcher in Houston.

Fifteen minutes later, Dean's white van pulled up alongside them and slowed down to match their pace. "Hey, Wayne," he said through the open window. "Flat tyre?"

"Hers," Wayne replied, nodding.

"Well, hop in," Dean told them, parking the van on the side of the road.

After Wayne and Dean had loaded the bicycles into the back of the van, Rhonda introduced herself to Dean, but he didn't really speak to her. He seemed distant and only said a few words to Wayne.

The last thing Rhonda saw when Dean Corll dropped her off at her father's house, as she was unloading her bicycle from the van, was a wooden box the size of two coffins...

CHAPTER 31

On the night of August 7th 1973, a Tuesday, Wayne Henley walked out of his mother's house in the Heights to find a commotion at Rhonda's father's place, three houses down the street. Wayne was with one of his friends, nineteen-year-old Timothy Kerley, and they could hear screaming and kicking sounds coming from the house where Rhonda lived.

Both teenagers started running down 23rd Street, their sneakers crunching on the crumbling tar road. It was around eleven o'clock and a blanket of low clouds was obscuring any illumination from the moon and stars.

Upon reaching the Williams residence, they watched as Rhonda came limping out of the front door and down three patio steps, onto a badly maintained patch of lawn. "Help me, please!" she cried in a hoarse voice. She was dressed in a black shoulderless top, a pair of blue jeans and leather sandals. The sound of dogs barking frantically was coming from the backyard of the property.

Wayne leapt over the low wooden fence separating the front lawn from the sidewalk and jogged to meet her halfway. From inside the house, Ben's voice thundered: "Yeah, fuck off, you little slut! And don't bother to come back, do you hear me?" Wayne could see his fat belly, swaying around in a faded vest, through the small rectangular kitchen window.

Rhonda fell into Wayne's arms. "My dad is drunk again," she said. "If you don't get me out of here, he is going to kill me for sure." By now, she was suffering from severe emotional and physical trauma, brought on by months of various forms of abuse. Her eyes were red from crying and there was a purple bruise on her right cheek, Wayne noticed.

"Don't worry, Rhonda girl," he told her. "I will protect you."

"I'm scared, Wayne," she moaned, hobbling toward the pedestrian gate alongside him.

"What happened to your foot?" he asked, frowning at her swollen left foot. "Your father?"

"No, that wasn't him. I cracked a few small bones on Sunday. A car drove over my foot in the mall's parking lot."

They reached the gate, where Timothy was waiting, and Wayne said. "Rhonda, this is Tim Kerley. We're here with his car." He pointed at a metallic-green Volkswagen in front of his mother's house, further up the street. "I just needed to fetch some stuff from my mom's place quickly. It's a good thing we heard you screaming in there."

Rhonda introduced herself to Tim and then asked, "Where are you going now?"

"We're on our way to Dean's place for a party," Wayne informed her. "Come on, let's get you away from here, girl."

After reluctantly agreeing, Rhonda accompanied them to Tim's Volkswagen and climbed in, settling on the backseat. "How do you know Dean?" she asked Tim once he had started the engine.

"I don't," Tim replied, shrugging his narrow shoulders, while staring at her bruised cheek in the rear view mirror. He had very short hair with a clean-shaven chin and he was ferociously chewing on gum, Rhonda observed.

"That's not very comforting," she replied.

Wayne, who was in the passenger seat, turned to face her and said, "Don't be so tense, girl. Dean is not even at his house. He's at a work party at that new pub on Evergreen Drive and I don't think he will be back until the early hours of the morning." He rolled down the window and lit a cigarette. "Are you okay?" he asked, staring through the Volkswagen's windshield.

"Not really," Rhonda replied, desperate for sympathy. "My dad punched me in the chest and I think I broke a rib or something."

"And your face?" Wayne wanted to know.

Rhonda ran a thumb over the bruise on her cheek. "That's from yesterday. He ripped my bedroom door off in yet another drunken fit and then he attacked me, but I managed to escape after the first blow. He also banned me from bringing any friends over in future." She sniffed and wiped tears from her eyes with her knuckles. "I can't take it anymore, Wayne."

"We need to get you someplace else to live," Wayne said. "You can stay over at Dean's house tonight and then we'll make another plan in the morning."

Tim briefly interrupted their conversation to ask for directions and then Rhonda shook her head while saying, "I don't know about staying over at an older man's house, Wayne. I don't really like Dean. He kind of freaks me out."

Wayne waved a dismissive hand. "No, he's cool. You'll see."

***

They arrived at 2020 Lamar Drive in Pasadena at close to midnight and Dean wasn't home yet.

Wayne put a Pink Floyd album on the stereo, then offered Rhonda and Tim beer from the bar fridge beneath the liquor cabinet in the lounge. After kicking off his shoes, he sat down on the carpet and grinned. "You won't believe what I brought," he said. Delving into the back pocket of his jeans, he retrieved a tiny plastic bag filled with a white powdery substance.

"Is that cocaine?" Tim asked nervously.

"The purest," Wayne confirmed. "All the way from Columbia, my friend." He poured the contents onto the smooth wooden surface of the coffee table and divided it into three lines with one of Dean Corll's many blank postcards.

While staring at the lines in disbelief, Rhonda said, "No way. I don't do hard drugs. You know that, Wayne."

"Well, you're gonna have to take something, girl. I mean, to get rid of all the suffering your dick of a dad put you through, you know?"

"Definitely not coke," Rhonda replied.

"Bagging then," Wayne suggested.

"Bagging?" she curiously echoed.

Tim looked at her and smiled. "What, you haven't done bagging before?"

Rhonda assured them that she had no idea what bagging was and Wayne went into the garage, through a door in the kitchen, to fetch a brown paper bag and a can of acrylic paint.

Upon returning to the lounge, he carefully transferred some paint from the can to the bag and then showed Rhonda how to inhale and exhale fumes using the bag, creating a massive rush of blood into her brain.

"Wow, that's better," she said in a dreamy voice. "It's almost like I can't even feel any pain anymore. This stuff really makes you high."

"That's my girl!" Wayne exclaimed.

He ended up snorting the three lines of cocaine all by himself and then the three of them shared a joint while chatting away, drinking more beer and dancing around in the lounge.

Dean Corll returned to his house a few minutes before two o'clock in the morning – fairly intoxicated from the amount of cocktails he had consumed at the company party – and he was instantly annoyed when Wayne introduced him to the two visitors.

"Can we have a word in private?" he said to his accomplice, who promptly followed him down the corridor and into the kitchen.

"What's wrong?" Wayne asked once Dean had closed the kitchen door behind them.

"Where the hell is David?" Dean countered.

"He's at home with his wife."

Dean pushed the youngster up against the refrigerator and said, "What the fuck do you think you're doing bringing a girl here?"

Wayne held his hands in the air, palms facing forward. "Forgive me, Dean. It's just… her father was drunk and he was beating her. We just had to get her out of there, man. Now, please lower your voice. I'm sure we can work something out."

"You know how I despise women," Dean said in a loud whisper. "You've ruined everything, Wayne. I want boys here, not whores. And that Tim buddy of yours in there is too old. I want young ones, like that Dreymala boy who was looking for empty bottles in the garage the other night." He released his grip on Wayne's shoulders and stood back. "I've had a long night, so I am going to bed now. When I wake up the other two better be gone, are we clear?"

"Yes, Dean," Wayne said. "Can we at least finish our drinks before they leave? We won't make a lot of noise, I promise."

"You do whatever you want to," Dean replied, pushing a finger under Wayne's nose, "but when I wake up tomorrow morning and find them still in my house, there's going to be trouble. I have to go to work early, all right?"

He went to his bedroom without speaking to the visitors again and Wayne returned to the lounge to explain the rules (as well as the fact that they could stay for a while longer) to his friends. They turned the music down a couple of notches, closed the door between the lounge and the corridor leading to the bedrooms, and then partied on as quietly as they could under the circumstances.

When their third round of Budweisers was finished, Tim fetched more from the kitchen, while Wayne poured whiskey chasers on the liquor cabinet.

"What does Dean do for a living anyway?" Rhonda asked, thinking about the wooden box she had seen in the back of his van a few days earlier.

"He's an electrician," Wayne answered, handing her a shot of whiskey, "at the power company."

Rhonda took the whiskey and poured it down her throat. "Why doesn't he like girls?"

Sitting down beside her, Wayne raised his eyebrows. "How do you know he does not like girls?"

"I overheard some of the stuff he said to you in the kitchen."

"He's gay, Rhonda."

"Oh," she said, fiddling with one of her fake silver earrings. "Why are you then always hanging out with him? You're not gay."

"It's complicated," Wayne told her.

Tim Kerley, who had returned from the kitchen with a six-pack of beers, didn't say a word. He did not know a thing about Wayne's situation with Dean Corll.

An hour later, the three teenagers were passed out on the carpet after hallucinating on paint fumes, smoking more weed, and consuming more alcohol.

CHAPTER 32

At six minutes past six o'clock, on the morning of August 8th 1973, Rhonda awoke with a massive headache and a sharp pain in her side as someone kicked her in the ribs, shouting, "Wake up, bitch!"

Her very first thought was that it was her father, Ben Williams.

But then she opened her eyes and figured out she was on the floor in someone else's house.

Through the sheer curtains, she could see that dawn was busy breaking outside. She was on her back with something hard pressing into her shoulder blades. Her hands were cuffed by cold metal handcuffs and her feet were bound together by something strong and tight. She found it difficult to breathe because her mouth was gagged, and the smell of stale smoke was filling her nostrils.

Turning her head to the left, Rhonda saw Wayne's friend, Tim Kerley, naked on his stomach and tied to the same plywood board she was bound to. His clothes lay in a rumpled heap behind him. Like hers, Tim's mouth was gagged and taped shut with duct tape. Underneath the plywood board was a large transparent plastic sheet covering a rust-colored carpet, she noticed.

Stay calm, Rhonda Williams silently told herself, while the fuzzy memories were slowly crawling back into her mind. *You are at Dean Corll's house and Wayne must be here somewhere. He will help you. Just stay calm.*

Recalling how Wayne had told her that Dean had gone to bed earlier, she now regretted sniffing more paint and drinking more beer and whiskey. She should have left then. She should have called someone to come fetch her. *Stay calm, Rhonda. Breathe deeply now.*

She gradually turned her head to the right and watched as Dean – dressed only in a pair of boxer shorts – hunched over Wayne Henley to remove a strip of duct tape from his mouth. Wayne was still in his jeans and t-shirt from the previous night and he was also handcuffed, with his feet tied together by thick nylon rope.

As soon as the adhesive tape wasn't covering his mouth anymore, Wayne cried, "What the hell, Dean? What are you doing?"

"Man, you blew everything bringing this girl here," Dean told him, kicking Rhonda hard in the chest. "I'm so fucking angry with you, Wayne! Today is the day I am teaching you a lesson."

Rhonda felt the air escape from her lungs and wanted to scream in agony, but her mouth was gagged so tightly that she could barely move her lips. Tears suddenly started rolling down her cheeks and her nose made an involuntary sniffing sound. *You are not going to die, Rhonda. Just remain calm.*

Looking up again, she stared into the eyes of the madman. They were black and glistening in the artificial light coming from a bed lamp in the corner of what she had now established was a bedroom.

"Dean, please," Wayne said in a small voice. "Please untie me."

"I'm gonna kill you all," Dean Corll huffed. "But first I am gonna have my fun with you!"

"Let me loose," Wayne kept on pleading. "If you untie me, I will help you kill them."

Rhonda couldn't believe what she was hearing. *Is Wayne really going to help the madman kill me and his friend or is he somehow trying to distract Dean to help us all escape*? She wasn't sure, but she was anxiously hoping it was the latter. Behind her, Tim was hysterically trying to free himself by writhing around, to no avail.

Dean stared at Wayne for a long minute, then said, "All right, Wayne, but if you try anything stupid I will send a bullet into your brain, do you understand me?"

"Y-yes, D-Dean," Wayne stuttered, his eyes rolling upward to look at the .22 caliber pistol on the bedside table.

Dean picked up the pistol, shoved it into the waistband of his boxers, then grabbed Wayne Henley by his shoulders and dragged him out of the room. A little while later, Rhonda could hear them speak in the kitchen. She knew this because Wayne had just warned Dean about the stove leaking gas.

"Forget about the damn stove," Dean said. "I am going to untie your feet first. If you try to run away, I'm going to shoot you in the back, so make sure you sit tight, pal."

Wayne didn't offer a reply.

"Are you going to help me torture them?" Dean asked. His voice had a cynical undertone in it.

"Yes, I am," Wayne said. "We're going to do this together, Dean."

Then the shock and confusion overpowered Rhonda Williams and she lost consciousness.

***

When she came to again, Rhonda saw how Dean walked into the bedroom with a transistor radio under his left arm and the shiny pistol clutched in his right hand. He placed the radio on the floor in the corner just as Wayne appeared in the doorway. He was still fully clothed and now untied, with an eighteen-inch hunting knife tucked into his cowboy belt. Outside, an orange sun was creeping over the eastern horizon and a slight breeze was picking up.

"Take care of her," Dean instructed before leaving the room once again.

Moments later, Wayne was crouched beside Rhonda Williams and removed the tape and the cotton gag from her mouth.

She lifted her head and asked in an unsteady voice, "Wayne, is this for real?"

"Yes, I'm afraid it is," he answered with the sour fumes of digested alcohol on his breath.

"Are you going to do anything about it?" Rhonda wanted to know.

Stroking her hair gently, Wayne whispered, "Everything is going to be okay, Rhonda. I'm gonna get you out of here, don't you worry."

As soon as Wayne stood up and started pacing around, Dean returned to the room. This time he was carrying a metal toolbox, which he put down next to the radio on the floor. Rhonda noticed him placing the gun on the nightstand by the door before removing his boxer shorts.

"Cut off Rhonda's clothes!" he told Wayne.

Wayne knelt down beside her and used the knife to first slice her jeans and then her panties into bits. When he was about to start on the shirt, Rhonda said, "Please don't, Wayne. It's my friend Sheila's top. You can take it off, but please don't ruin it?" *Why is he doing this*? she wondered in a panic.

After a nod of approval from Dean, Wayne put the knife down and took her shirt and bra off without cutting them. Now, poor Rhonda was nude and exposed. She felt violated and ashamed.

"Come with me," Dean Corll ordered.

Following him out of the room, Wayne looked back and mouthed, "It's gonna be okay."

When they were out of sight, Rhonda turned her head to face Tim Kerley and whispered, "Wayne is going to rescue us, just play along, all right?"

Tim gave her a look that said, *Are you out of your mind*?

Dean returned three minutes later, shadowed by Wayne, and he cleared his throat before announcing: "Here's what's going to happen now, boys and girls. Wayne is going to have sex with you, Rhonda, while I'm going to enjoy young Timothy over there. Then we are going to murder the both of you."

While Dean slowly approached Tim Kerley, whose eyes were bewildered with fear, Wayne asked, "Dean, can I please take Rhonda into the room next door?"

"No!" Dean barked. "You will do it in here. Take off your pants. Now!"

Instead of reaching for his belt or his zipper, Wayne Henley was gazing back and forth between Rhonda on the floor and the nightstand with the gun resting on it. Then, on pure impulse, he darted to the nightstand and grasped the .22 pistol in both hands.

Pointing the gun at Dean Corll, he took three steps back and shouted, "You've gone far enough, Dean! I can't go on any longer! I can't have you kill any more of my friends!"

Dean moved away from Tim Kerley and walked sideways in the direction of the door, his hands on his hips. "Come on, kill me, Wayne!" he said loudly. "You won't do it!"

Wayne stepped back another two paces. "Yes, I will. I can and I will. It's over, man."

"You won't do it!" Dean repeated, even louder this time. He was now almost in the doorway.

Rhonda was holding her breath but she didn't close her eyes.

Wayne Henley pulled the trigger.

The bullet hit Dean in the side of his head and he staggered through the doorway and into the corridor. He was screaming in anguish when Wayne fired two more shots, both penetrating his left shoulder. Striking the wall of the hallway with a thud, his body twisted violently and then he began to slump to the floor. Wayne fired three more shots into his lower back, until the Candy Man's naked body finally ended up stretched out sideways on the laminated corridor floor, facing the wall. A pool of dark red blood was gathering underneath the torso.

Dean Corll was dead.

The deadliest serial killer in American history could never murder another teenage boy again.

Other than the quiet, rhythmic sobs coming from Rhonda Williams, there was silence in the house on Lamar Drive.

CHAPTER 33

Wayne first attended to Rhonda before helping his friend, Tim Kerley.

He kept on asking, "Are you okay? Are you okay?" while wrapping a blanket around her fragile body.

Rhonda opened her mouth to speak, but the words wouldn't come out. She was trembling with fear and her mind was in a haze. Wayne untied her feet and uncuffed her with the keys he'd found on the bedside table. Then he went over to Tim, removed the tape from his mouth and untied him from Dean's torture board as well.

"Thank you, Wayne!" Tim exclaimed, hugging his friend. "You saved our lives! Thank you so much!" He reached for his clothes and began to pull on his jeans.

Composing herself, Rhonda put on her bra and top while looking at an electronic clock on the nightstand: 7:57 a.m. She stood up and hugged the blanket around her bruised body. "What on earth do we do now?" she asked in a low-pitched tone.

"We're getting out of here," Wayne replied. He was staring at Dean's corpse in the corridor.

"No, we should call the police," Tim suggested. "Our fingerprints are all over the place, man."

Wayne thought about this for a moment, then said, "Yeah, you're probably right."

The three of them cautiously stepped over Dean Corll's bloodied body and went into the lounge, where Wayne found a telephone directory in the stationary cabinet.

Walking to the front door with wobbly legs, he picked up the telephone receiver on the wall beside the key holder and dialled the number.

"This is the Pasadena Police Department," a female operator answered. "How can we help?"

"Y'all better come here right now!" Wayne blurted out. "I just killed a man!" Reality had now kicked in and he was completely panic-stricken.

"May I have your name, please?" the police operator asked calmly.

"Elmer Wayne Henley!" he said.

"What's the address?"

"It's two zero two zero Lamar Drive," Wayne told her. His vision was blurred, his head was pounding and his mouth was dry.

"We'll dispatch someone right away," the operator said. "Just wait there."

After he'd hung up, they all went outside and sat on the porch steps while waiting for the police to arrive. Rhonda was now wearing the blanket like a sarong, wrapped around her legs and tied in a bulging knot at the waist. Wayne and Tim had their jeans and t-shirts on, without any shoes.

They sat in silence for a number of minutes, until Tim turned to Wayne and said, "Damn it, Wayne! I can't believe you just shot him dead like that. It was insane, man!"

"I've done that four or five times already," Wayne replied absently.

"What?"

"I'm going to jail, Tim." Wayne said. He lit a Marlboro and inhaled deeply. "You know, if you weren't my friend, I could have gotten two hundred dollars for you."

Tim Kerley only shook his head in perplexity.

***

Patrolman A.B. Jamison arrived at 2020 Lamar Drive on Wednesday August 8th at 8:32 a.m.

The previous night's cloud cover had disappeared and he was surprised to see three teenagers sitting on the porch outside the house. The operator who'd taken the call had informed him that a "young man" had placed it.

Jamison climbed out of the car and approached the teenagers, carefully scanning the surroundings, while shielding his eyes from the sun with his forearm. The house was a green-and-white framed bungalow in need of paintwork and general reparations. A large tree stood in the center of the front lawn, casting a fat shadow over the porch where the youths were sitting. Nothing seemed suspicious or out of place.

"Who is the individual who placed the call to the station?" he asked upon reaching the porch steps.

One of the boys stood up and said, "That would be me, sir. Elmer Wayne Henley."

"Can you describe what happened here, Mr Henley?"

"I shot a man. His name was Dean Corll."

"Where is he now?" Jamison asked.

"Inside the house," Wayne replied, pointing at the front door with his index finger.

"Is there anyone else inside, Mr Henley?"

"No, sir. Just the dead body."

Officer Jamison escorted the three teenagers to his patrol car where he told them to wait inside the vehicle while he inspected the property.

When he walked into the bungalow and discovered the corpse, Jamison made the following notes in his little black book:

- Muscular male, mid-thirties, naked on floor in hallway
- Over six feet tall, weighing approximately 200 pounds
- Dark brown hair, graying at the temples
- Gunshot wounds to the head (1), left shoulder (2) and lower back (3)
- No breathing, no pulse

He then called for backup on his radio and returned to his patrol car in the driveway.

After instructing Wayne Henley to step out of the vehicle, Jamison said, "Elmer Wayne Henley, you have the right to remain silent. Anything you say, can and will be used against you in a court of law. You have the right to speak to an attorney, and to have an attorney present during any questioning. If you cannot afford a lawyer, one will be provided for you at government expense."

When he was finished, Wayne shouted: "I don't care who knows about it! I have to get it off my chest!" He clutched his head and began to cry. "I'm done living a lie. I want to make things right." Shaking his head, he got back into the patrol car.

The moment a team of detectives arrived, Officer Jamison handed the crime scene over to them and then drove the three teenagers to the police station for questioning.

The detectives processed the scene and found that the carpeted floor in the master bedroom was covered in thick plastic sheeting and appeared to be rigged up for some kind of sick ceremony.

There was a plywood board, measuring eight by three feet, with handcuffs attached to two corners and nylon ropes to the other two. They also found a .22 caliber pistol, a bayonet-like knife, duct tape, rolls of clear plastic of the same type used to cover the floor, eight pairs of handcuffs, a number of rubber dildos, thin glass tubes, petroleum jelly, a whip and more lengths of nylon rope.

In the Ford Econoline van, parked in the driveway, they found a coil of rope, a dirty rug and a wooden crate containing several strands of human hair.

It was one of the strangest sights the team of Pasadena detectives had ever seen.

34
CHAPTER

A stocky police detective with cropped brown hair walked into the cramped little custody room at the Pasadena Police Department with a tape recorder in his hands. Wayne Henley looked up from where he was sitting, behind an old teak table, and watched as the officer eased the door shut behind him. There was no air-conditioning and the custody room felt like a sauna in the summer heat.

Placing the recorder down on the table, the detective straightened his uniform, then sat down across from Wayne and folded his hands on the table.

After a long uncomfortable silence, he finally pressed the record button and said in a formal voice: "August, eighth, nineteen-seventy-three, ten fifteen in the a.m. Interrogation of Elmer Wayne Henley, age seventeen, prime suspect in the murder of Dean Arnold Corll, a thirty-three-year-old electrician from Pasadena." He paused to sit back in his chair and then continued: "Mr Henley, did you place a call to the police station shortly after eight this morning, stating that you have killed a man?"

Wayne slowly licked his dry lips and then replied, "Yes, I did, sir."

"And was the name of the man you were referring to Dean Corll?"

"Yes it was."

"And how exactly did you kill Mr Corll, Mr Henley?"

"I shot him six times with his own pistol," Wayne said, shuddering at his recollection.

"And why did you do that?"

"I acted in self-defense."

The detective frowned. "Self-defense?"

"Am I allowed to smoke in here?" Wayne Henley asked, retrieving a packet of Marlboros from the front pocket of his jeans.

"No, you're not," replied the detective.

Wayne put the cigarettes down on the table in frustration, staring at his interrogator. "May I at least have a glass of water, please?"

The officer left the room without answering and returned a short while later, holding a paper cup filled with lukewarm water. After handing the cup to Wayne, he pressed pause on the tape recorder and said, "Look, this doesn't mean that you're calling the shots, tough guy. The fact that I'm giving you something to drink is only to show you that I'm treating you like a human being."

While Wayne was gulping down the disgusting tap water, the detective reactivated the recording and said, "Mr Henley, can you elaborate on the self-defense statement you have made earlier?"

Pushing his wavy hair back over his scalp with both hands, Wayne said, "It's a long story, sir."

"We have all day, Mr Henley. Let's start with how you ended up at Mr Corll's house this morning."

"It goes back way further than that," Wayne replied. He could hear the tremble in his own voice.

"We'll talk about that later," the detective told him, "let us first start with how you and your two friends ended up at Mr Corll's address this morning."

"Last night," Wayne corrected him. "We slept over."

"All right then, Mr Henley, last night. Start with last night."

Wayne explained how he and Dean had an arrangement whereby he could come and go to the house on Lamar Drive as he pleased, and that he even owned a key to the bungalow. He then described the previous night's party, Dean's return and subsequent anger about Rhonda Williams being there, and how they had all woken up tied up and cuffed early in the morning.

"I eventually convinced Dean to set me free…" Wayne concluded, catching his breath, "…which he did, but then he threatened to kill all of us, so I had to kill him first."

The officer shook his head at how easy the confession was coming from the teenager and then asked, "How long have you known Mr Corll?"

"About two years now," Wayne answered, wiping sweat from his brow with his dirty t-shirt. Then his emotional walls suddenly shattered to pieces. He simply couldn't live a lie anymore. Jumping to his feet, he began to scratch his arms and chest in agitation. "We killed several boys!" he blurted out in a loud, grunting voice.

"What did you say?" replied the detective.

"Dean and Dave and I," Wayne clarified. "We killed them missing boys from Houston Heights."

"Dave? Who's Dave? I thought your friend's name was Timothy."

Wayne slumped down into the armchair again. "Dave… David Brooks. He is the one who introduced me to Dean Corll back in nineteen-seventy-one. It was our job to procure the boys for Dean. At first, we thought they were being sold to a homosexual slavery organization in Dallas, but later we learned that Dean raped and killed them…" Wayne's voice trailed off and his chin shamefully dropped to his chest. "Then we began to assist him for money."

"Assist him? In raping the boys?"

"No, we never did any of that stuff, only Dean did. We helped with the killings and the burying of the bodies."

"How many boys are we talking about exactly?" asked the detective. His face was white as snow.

"A lot," Wayne replied, tears now streaming down his cheeks. "I don't know the exact number, but I actively participated in the torture and murder of at least six or seven of them."

The interrogating detective couldn't comprehend what he was hearing. He was stunned into silence. A clock against the wall was ticking away the seconds while he tried to recall all the missing person's cases some of his colleagues over at Houston Heights had been trying to solve recently.

A while later, when Wayne wasn't asked any further questions, he said, "Sir, I know where the bodies are buried. I can take you there now if you want me to."

"Let me call David Mullican," the detective mumbled. "Now that we have multiple murders, he is going to take over as the chief investigating officer."

***

They arrived at Dean Corll's boatshed in Southwest Houston shortly after one o'clock in the afternoon. A clutter of television news reporters was already gathered outside, in the blazing heat, after the story had leaked from an unknown source inside the Pasadena Police Department.

By then, Detective Mullican, from the Houston Police Department, had spoken to the three interrogating officers and established that the statements given by Tim Kerley and Rhonda Williams corroborated Wayne's story about shooting Dean Corll in self-defense.

He quickly briefed his team on site about the background on the case and then instructed them to get to work on Corll's metal boat shed.

After forcefully removing the lock on the shed's door with a pair of industrial bolt cutters, Detective Larry Earls – the assistant investigating officer – entered the stuffy, windowless stall and ordered four prison trustees to roll the half-stripped car out of there to create floor space for the digging.

Wayne Henley was watching from about twenty feet away, where he was standing between two plainclothes police officers.

"Where should we commence the excavation, Mr Henley?" Lieutenant Breck Porter – a meticulous homicide detective from Houston PD – asked, staring at a plastic bag filled with clothing in one corner of the shed. He was in uniform, with his cowboy-style police hat covering his receding hairline, the front of the hat almost resting on the top of his horn-rimmed eyeglasses.

Wayne swallowed hard. "Anywhere, sir. They are pretty much all over the place." He clenched his pale jaw and then added, "I mean, the bodies cover the entire floor area inside the stall."

The prison trustees began to dig next to the western wall and found the first dead body, covered in plastic sheeting and lime powder, within minutes.

They continued ploughing into the soil of the dry-land marina until well into the evening, finding corpse after corpse, all of them the remains of teenage boys, in various stages of decomposition. Every now and again someone would shout, "Here's another one!" Then the cadaver of yet another deceased youth would be added to the mounting heap of bodies in front of the boat shed.

All of the bodies were naked, some of them had rags in their mouths, some were bound, some had ligatures still tied around the necks, and a few had bullet wounds in the skulls. Deeper down, the bodies had decomposed to such an extent that only skeletons remained. The police officers and news reporters at the scene were struggling to keep their composure. Detective Larry Earls chain-smoked a packet of twenties down to zero within five hours, in an attempt to drive away the overpowering stench.

The atmosphere was sombre, yet extremely tense; almost paranormal.

While this was going on, Breck Porter spoke to the owner of the boat storage facility, Mrs. Meynier, who told him what a gentlemen Dean Corll was. She said that he had rented the place for nearly three years, that he always settled his bills on time, and that he usually visited the stall once or twice a week. She also stated that Corll had been inquiring about renting an additional shed two weeks earlier, because his number eleven shed was "getting full".

At a stage, an ABC13 news reporter interviewed Lieutenant Porter and asked him what his take was on the whole mess. "Well, it's just horrible," he said. "If you're talking about a sadistic pervert like this, you can expect mostly anything. They used all kinds of instruments and a sexual torture rack on the boys before murdering them."

The same reporter also interviewed Wayne Henley, where he was now sitting in the back of one of the police vehicles with the door open. "Dean wanted to kill me," Wayne said, sucking on a cigarette. "He was mad because I brought the chick over there. I thought it was safe to take her to Dean's house. I didn't know any better."

"But now he cannot kill anymore boys," the reporter said, sounding sympathetic.

"I know," Wayne replied, "but it was still all my fault. I can't help but feel guilty."

"Why is that?"

"Because I introduced Dean to them boys. I caused them to be dead."

Later that evening, David Owen Brooks, accompanied by his father, arrived at the Houston Police Station where he denied any involvement in the murders, but confessed to having knowledge of what Dean Corll, The Candy Man, had done. He also admitted to being aware of Corll's boat shed and by his estimation he thought that the police would find "between eight and ten bodies over there".

His figures weren't even close.

In the end, a staggering seventeen bodies were recovered from underneath shed number eleven at the *Southwest Boat Storage* facility on Silver Bell Street.

CHAPTER 35

THE LARGEST MULTIPLE MURDER CASE IN UNITED STATES HISTORY was the headline on the front page of the *New York Times* newspaper the next morning.

Although the term "serial killer" had not yet been in use, everybody in America knew about what was now referred to on television news as the Houston Mass Murders, committed by the most prolific killer in the country's history. Dean was referred to as "The Candy Man" or "The Pied Piper".

What most people couldn't understand was how it had been possible for so many boys to disappear from a single Houston neighborhood, a mere two miles wide and three miles deep, without the authorities figuring out that something was terribly wrong. The parents of the missing teenage boys were distraught and kept on phoning the police station in a panic to find out whether any of the bodies from the shed had been identified yet.

Wayne Henley, who had restlessly slept on a filthy mattress in a holding cell at the Houston Police Station the previous night, received his wakeup call at 6:15 a.m.

He was asked to make a formal written statement, in which he admitted to him and David assisting Dean Corll in abducting and murdering "numerous youths". He further stated that the killings were in most cases performed by means of strangulation or by shooting the victims at one of Dean's many rental homes. In conclusion, Wayne wrote that the only three murders that David Brooks hadn't been involved in, were the last three during the summer of '73.

When he was escorted to a marked police vehicle outside, half an hour later, Wayne wasn't surprized to see his old friend, David, dressed in shorts and a vest, standing beside the patrol car, in custody. He was, however, surprised to learn that David Brooks had turned *himself* in to the authorities; that he hadn't been arrested because Wayne had named him in the interview the day before.

"Good morning, Mr Henley," said Detective Mullican, his voice edgy. "I believe you have met David Brooks over here. He has informed us that there are more dead bodies at Lake Sam Rayburn and at High Island Beach. Is that true?"

"Yes," Wayne replied. "Yes it is."

They drove with the police to Dean's stepfather's cabin at the lake and then David began to point out the locations of the shallow graves where four victims had been buried in the woods, close to a water reservoir. Once again, there was a strong media presence and Detective Mullican was forced to assign two officers just to keep them at bay.

By the time the police exhumed the fourth body, David Brooks broke into tears. "I cannot take this anymore," he wailed, getting into one of the police vehicles while holding his head in his hands.

Detective Mullican allowed Wayne – who was becoming a hero in the eyes of the media because he had killed the monster, Dean Corll – to speak to news reporters once again. "These were just some boys we picked up with Dean," Wayne said, staring at the four lime-covered corpses, wrapped in plastic sheeting on the ground. "He raped them and then he killed them and then we brought them down here and buried them."

"What part did you play in the raping and the killing of these boys?" the ABC13 news reporter asked, waving a scourge of mosquitos away with his left hand.

"No comment," Wayne replied, not looking up at the video camera. His hands were shaking, his hair was a tangled mess and he was still dressed in the same dirty clothing he had worn the previous day.

The reporter gave a sigh. "Wayne, this has been going on for some time, hasn't it?"

"About a year ago last winter."

"That was when you got into it?"

Wayne thought about this for a moment, then said, "Yeah, that's right."

"Do you know if Dean Corll was involved in this earlier than that?"

"I know it for sure," Wayne replied. Behind them, Detective Mullican was instructing a forensic investigator to photograph the bodies.

"In what way do you know?" the news reporter asked, scribbling something down in his notepad.

"I was told, by Dean himself and by David Brooks."

The reporter consulted his notes. "And this David Brooks is another person that has been named as a suspect. What role did he play in all of this?"

"The same as mine," Wayne Henley answered, his voice barely above a whisper. Then he turned and climbed into the nearest police vehicle.

***

Later that afternoon, Wayne and David accompanied Detective Mullican and his investigative team to High Island Beach, where they pointed out five more sandy graves in extremely windy conditions. This time, in addition to the media, hundreds of Texas citizens were there to observe the spectacle of digging up the bodies, as the tide was turning from high to low.

Upon Wayne Henley's suggestion that there should be six corpses buried on the beach, not only five, the police ordered a NASA helicopter (equipped with sophisticated infrared scanners) to find the sixth body, about two miles north of the protruding boulder where the other bodies had been exhumed.

The television news reporters were once again allowed to speak to Wayne, who said that he wanted to correct certain statements he had read in the newspapers. David was sitting on the backseat of a patrol car and it seemed like he and Wayne Henley were not on speaking terms at that stage.

"I didn't implicate David Brooks like they said in the newspapers," Wayne told one of the reporters, this time looking straight into the camera. "I only made my official statement this morning, after Dave made his statement last night. He implicated himself. And I never said there were thirty bodies; I said twenty-four. That is all I want to tell you."

After the police had loaded the six corpses in a coroner's van, Detective Mullican chased the news reporters away, then called Wayne and David aside and asked, "Are these all the bodies that you two know of?" He tucked his thumbs into his belt and waited impatiently for an answer.

Nodding slowly, Wayne said, "I believe so, sir."

But David shook his head in disagreement. "There's one more, Mr Mullican," he confessed, while the wind was blowing his hair into his face. "He is buried at Jefferson County Beach."

When Wayne stared at him sceptically, David pushed his glasses up the bridge of his nose and mumbled: "You don't know about him, Wayne. He was one of my best friends, Joseph Lyles. Dean killed him after he put up a fight when Dean was still living in Spring Branch. That was some time in February this year."

This was news to Wayne Henley. He was under the impression that he'd been involved in all the murders between September 1971 and August 1973.

***

Once the police had exhumed the body of Joseph Lyles at Jefferson County Beach, the total tally of dead boys came to an astounding twenty-eight.

The Houston community was shocked beyond belief and the story stayed on the front pages of local papers for nearly four weeks.

Most of the victims were only identified months or years later, as and when more reliable proofing methods such as DNA testing became available.

CHAPTER 36

In search of more bodies, the police dug up the backyard of 2020 Lamar Drive as well as the area behind the old *Corll Candy Company*'s factory building in Houston Heights.

After finding nothing at these two locations, the Chambers County sheriff called off the excavations, despite the fact that many people reckoned Dean Corll could have murdered more teenagers; murders that David and Wayne perhaps didn't know about. The total number of boys who had gone missing from the Houston area between 1970 and 1973 was forty-two.

A grand jury convened on August 13th 1973 to hear evidence against Wayne Henley, David Brooks and Dean Corll.

The two main witnesses to testify were Timothy Kerley and Rhonda Williams but there was also another teenager, Billy Ridinger, who had something to say about Dean Corll and his accomplices. Apparently he had escaped death while Dean had been living in Schuler Street. According to Ridinger's testimony, Wayne, David and Dean lured him to the house with the promise of free beer and marijuana. He was then tied to the plywood torture board (which he described in detail without having access to any of the photos the police had taken) and abused by Dean Corll. David Brooks eventually persuaded Dean to release Billy Ridinger, which the Candy Man did. When Billy was asked by the jury why he didn't go to the police after the incident, he answered, "I was too scared he would come after me again and I felt too humiliated to speak to anyone about it."

The grand jury eventually indicted David Brooks on four murder counts and Wayne Henley on six. Bail was set at a hundred thousand dollars for each of them. Wayne wasn't charged for killing Dean. It was rated to be a justifiable homicide.

Dean Corll was found unimputable by death.

Following the indictments, Governor Dolph Briscoe appeared on television news, urging all teenage runaways in Texas to call their parents and let them know that they were safe, while Walter Mondale, a senator from Minnesota, asked Congress to allocate thirty million dollars to establish nationwide halfway houses for runaway teenagers.

Amongst Dean Corll's belongings, found in his Pasadena home, was a sex-education textbook used across all Texas schools – *Human Sexuality*, written by a University of Houston psychology professor, James Leslie McCary. When a California legislator found out about this, he wrote a letter to Governor Ronald Reagan, asking him to withdraw the book from America's schools, because it advocated that homosexuality was not an abnormal behaviour. In those days, there was a general misconception that homosexuality automatically implied paedophilia.

The legislator wrote the following to Reagan: *Perhaps you should take a trip down to Texas and ask the parents of the young boys if the unusual sexual expressions Dean Corll engaged in should be considered abnormal.*

***

David Brooks and Wayne Henley were tried separately for their respective roles in the shocking Houston Mass Murders.

Wayne's trial started in San Antonio on July 1st 1974.

Once again Rhonda, Tim and Billy Ridinger testified for the State of Texas, like they had done before the grand jury in the indictments. Wayne did not take the stand on advice from his attorney, who cross-examined some of the State witnesses but did not introduce any witnesses for the defense.

Evidence introduced to the court included the plywood board, torture instruments, handcuffs, nylon rope, duct tape, Dean's toolbox and the wooden box used to transport the bodies. By the time the trial was underway, forensic examiners had concluded that some of the strands of hair inside the box belonged to Charles Cobble, Dean Corll's twenty-seventh victim.

Former employees of *Corll Candy Company* testified that Dean had procured rolls of clear plastic of exactly the same type used to wrap his victims in, while a number of his co-workers at the *Houston Lighting and Power Company* stated that he had always taken coils of nylon cord (discarded by the power utility because of poor quality) home with him. The brand of this cord was the same type found on many of the bodies he had buried.

After closing arguments had been delivered two weeks later, on July 15th, the jury deliberated for an hour and a half before finding Elmer Wayne Henley guilty on all six murder charges.

Three weeks later, Judge Preston Dial sentenced him to ninety-nine years in prison for each of the convictions. The terms were to be served consecutively.

David's trial only began late in the winter of 1975, on February 27th.

His attorney argued that he hadn't committed any murders and told the court that Dean Corll and Wayne Henley were the only active participants in the torture and the killings.

In reply to this, Assistant District Attorney Tommy Dunn said to the jury: "The defendant was in on this murderous rampage from the very beginning. He tells you he was a cheerleader if nothing else. That's what he was telling you about his presence. But you know he was in on it."

The same as in Wayne's case, the jury only needed ninety minutes of deliberation to reach a guilty verdict against David Owen Brooks. He was sentenced to life imprisonment.

***

An interesting but staggering development followed a month later, in March 1975.

The Houston Police Department was busy with a routine investigation at an abandoned house in The Heights when they found a stash of homosexual pornographic films and pictures, featuring teenage boys. Much to the shock of the investigators, they discovered that eleven of the sixteen boys depicted in the photos and videos were victims of Dean Corll. This disturbing finding was possible proof that Corll had, in fact, belonged to a sexual slavery organization prior to recruiting David and Wayne. Furthermore, the stash led investigators to California – the state where Dean had told David the boys had been sent to – where they arrested five men in Santa Clara.

The police didn't know whether Dean Corll had ever solicited any boys using an organization, before Wayne and David came into the picture, because they both testified that Dean had never talked about any names of other people involved. It was decided not to pursue the matter further since the families of the victims had "suffered enough".

Nevertheless, when David Brooks found out about the arrest in Santa Clara, he told fellow prison inmates that Dean had revealed to him that the first boy he had killed, had been buried in the state of California.

Shortly after this revelation, an anonymous homosexual young man also came forward to speak about the Pied Piper.

Only referring to himself as "Guy", he told news reporters that Dean Corll had made sexual advances toward him in a public toilet at the mall. "I just wasn't interested at all," he said. "We became extremely close friends." Guy then went on to say that Dean was particularly kind to him, but that there was one bedroom in the house that was off limits to Guy. "I'll never take you in there," Dean had said to him. Guy also stated that Dean didn't like to go to openly gay bars and bathhouses because he wanted to stay underneath the radar as far as his sexual orientation was concerned.

Never in the time that they saw each other, did Guy notice any signs of violence from Dean Corll. "He was sort of like a cloud of mystique; he was just there. It seemed like he had another life he would go to and I was not a part of it, and I never wanted to infiltrate his other domain. He seemed to set up a barrier and wanted me to stay on one side. The other aspects of his life were taboo. I knew he had a friend named Wayne, but every time I'd bring up his friends, he'd more or less just cut them off. He never wanted me to meet them."

Guy said that Dean once told him: "Nobody loves you when you're old and gay." Then he made a suggestion for Guy to join him in getting away from Houston and moving to a place where nobody knew them, like South America.

Had Dean gone through with this plan, a strong possibility exists that twenty-eight or more Houston Heights boys would never have lost their lives...

***

"How that man was able to go out to that storage shed, time after time, and bury one more dead boy is something I'll never understand. You get close to evil like that, no matter how long ago it was, and it never leaves you."

Detective David Mullican, recollecting the Houston Mass Murders, April 2011

ABOUT THE AUTHOR

Robert Brown is an author and former freelance journalist in is mid-forties from California. Having been born and raised in the UK he moved to the US as a teenager with his family.

Robert moved back to the UK to pursue his dream to be a fulltime author. He lives in Liverpool with his wife and two children.

Robert has always been intrigued by true crime which led in part to his previous career of a freelance journalist writing for local publications primarily about unsolved murders. It was obvious to Robert that his passion for this genre would lead to him writing his first book "Deadly Illusions" in 2017.

Apart from writing Robert loves to spend time with his family and to indulge his other passion of the great outdoors. Having been raised in the UK it's no surprise that Robert is also a keen anglophile which is also reflected in his writing.

Robert has a unique writing style that uses both his UK and US backgrounds that creates stories that can be enjoyed by readers on both sides of the pond. Keep an eye out for further publications from Robert soon.

MORE BOOKS BY ROBERT BROWN

Deadly Illusions: A Private Detective Crime Thriller

Purity Pursuit: A Gripping Crime Thriller (Private Detective Heinrich Muller Crime Thriller Book 1)

Beyond The Window: A Fast Paced Crime Thriller (Private Detective Heinrich Muller Crime Thriller Book 2)

Stolen Heritage: Gripping Crime Thriller (Private Detective Heinrich Muller Crime Thriller Book 3)

The People In The Woods: Fast Paced Crime Thriller

Blood Money: Page Turning Crime Thriller

Private Detective Heinrich Muller Collection

The Numbers Game: A Crime and Mystery Thriller

Bonfire Bodies: A Terrifying True Crime Story: The Shocking Story of Serial Killer Dennis Nilsen

Printed in Great Britain
by Amazon